THE "S"WORD AND MORE BS

FIGHT LIKE JESUS

"IT IS WRITTEN"
"IT IS WRITTEN"
"IT IS WRITTEN"

A 40-DAY DEVOTIONAL

BY JOY ELLIOTT

ISBN: 9780982666555
RELIGION / CHRISTIAN LIFE / DEVOTIONAL

Published by PCG Legacy, a division of Pilot Communications Group, Inc.
317 Appaloosa Trail Waco, TX 76712
www.thepublishinghub.com

HOW TO REACH JOY ELLIOTT:
joyelliott@me.com

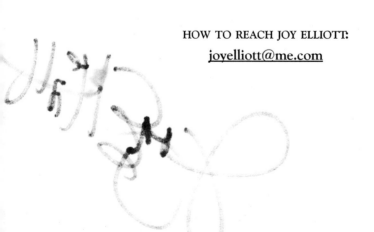

To my family & friends

There are very few people who know everything about you and still love you anyway. For those few who really know me and still love me, THANK YOU! As you all know, I haven't arrived yet (hence this book), but I am hoping you are enjoying the process with me as much as I am with you.

To my MAN, Lin Elliott, you are constant, the steady ship I get to dwell with on this unpredictable sea we call life. Your humor is my medicine. I LOVE being the woman married to YOU. Emily, my sweet angel, you are a continual reminder that God is so faithful. Your wisdom surpasses your years. Lil' Remi, you have this unique way of communicating to me things I believe God is showing me. God gave you an amazing voice and healing hands to use for His glory. Dad, thank you for pouring into me a foundation of truth and teaching me about the "volume of the Book." Mom, you are my loudest, proudest cheerleader, thanks for never dropping your pom-poms. To my in-laws, Margaret and Lindley, thank you for being the village that is constantly helping to raise our family. To all my other family members, I'll thank you at the next kick-ball game.

To my "oxygen mask" during this whole project, Marianne Cox, thank you for not letting me let this dream suffocate. Thank you for all the prayers, coffee shop talks, emails, phone calls, hours spent reading and correcting, and most importantly, all the encouragement! David Byrd, the instigator, thank you for teaching me about life's lessons and for pushing me beyond my comfort zone to complete this book. You will smile as you see they are woven throughout this book. A big hug goes out to my church family at First United Methodist Church of Waco. Brian Mast, Vern Herschberger, and Suzy Wright, a gigantic applause goes out to each one of you for all your AMAZING talent. To the rest of my really rockin' friends, you know who you are, I'll never forget all the s-Words and more BS we have shared together!

Contents

Introduction

The s-Word, the way I use it, is also known as "the sword" among BS-ing (Bible-studying) Christians. According to scripture, the sword happens to be the words of God written in the Bible and the words from the Spirit of God spoken to our hearts.

Words have taken me to the mountaintops, then straight down into the valleys of life and everywhere in between. Whether a word came from the s-Word (Bible), a family member, a friend, a foe, a book, or an advertisement, words have always moved me. Words strike a match in my soul to move me either for good or for bad. Words ignite a passion, a fury, a heated wave of emotions. Actions, thoughts, attractions, distractions — words bring about some form of reaction. Words are what unite us or divide us. Words bring life or death. Words create. This world called Earth was created by God's words!

I wrote this book because I wanted to learn to fight like Jesus! Anyone who can live a pure life on this earth, be tortured by others, and then nailed to a cross, only to rise again in three days, is someone I want to learn something from.

Jesus' first temptation was food, also a valid physical need and desire. (By the way, food was Eve's first temptation as well.) The next temptation Satan offered Jesus was to get God to "prove himself," and the third temptation was to take a shortcut in his life and abandon the will of God. With each temptation, Jesus said, "It is written." Jesus understood that the only weapon he had to fight his enemy (and our enemy) was the s-Word [words written in the Bible] and the Holy Spirit.

I went on this journey of writing this devotional book for myself to use daily for different seasons in my life. My hope is that it will transform your life as much as it has mine.

The Sense of Humor Spot

In every day's devotional, I begin with something that makes me laugh or smile. This was a must for me. (I tend to get a little uptight ... my husband doesn't call me "Gunny" for no reason.) A little militant I may be, but I love to laugh! Life has some tough issues, and even those issues have issues. A little laughter helps relieve the need for all those tissues.

WORD

This part of the devotional is a short story that applies to my life and explains what I learned from the Bible. (Well, most of the time I learn, but I do have a tendency to be a little stubborn. OK, so sometimes I want to learn, but I have to keep going to take the class over and over again. I know you know what I mean). The WORD sections of each daily devotional are meant to encourage you and me both to see life lessons and learn from them!

COME WITH ME TO THIS SCRIPTURE

This section of the devotional is us — you and me — going into scripture together. The scripture is set apart in a bold font; the regular-font words are just my words and my thoughts on what I believe I learned from that scripture. This section will hopefully be enlightening and thought provoking.

WHAT I LEARNED:

We must then ask ourselves, "What did I learn?" This question is so important for me to ask myself and answer in writing; otherwise, I just learn something and then it's gone! We are all so saturated with information, but if we write down what we learned, we tend to ponder it a little longer. We can really test if we understand what we just read.

YOUR TURN IN THE WORD:

Don't get scared! Get excited! This is your chance to open your Bible! If you are like me, you still have to go to the front of the Bible and find some of the books of the Bible in the Table of Contents, look at the page number that book starts on, and then go to it. How many times have I found myself not wanting to even open a Bible in a Bible study because I didn't want the other ladies to know I had no idea where to find Obadiah. Open your Bible!!! You're just getting started. You are going to learn so much. Let's let go of our pride together and fight like Jesus! Turn to the scripture references mentioned in the questions, and then fill in the blanks. Those blank lines following the scripture are for you to write any thoughts you may have about that scripture.

Thinking of Others ...

Now this is the best part — truly! If you understand nothing else in this book, understand this: True happiness and freedom come from praying, thinking, taking action, loving, and giving to others. Doing these things takes my mind off of me, and it focuses me on others. That in itself has set me free from self-destructive behavior and thoughts. This part of the devotional helps us to apply what we've learned toward blessing our family, our friends, our enemies (yes, we have to pray for them, too), and even people we don't know.

Repentance ...

Ouch, huh? Trust me; this is a good thing, even if painful at times! But repentance is not just admitting your wrong choices (sin) and living in sorrow. This section is for you to write down where you messed up and decide what steps you can take to change your thoughts, actions, words. Thoughts, actions, and words, if they go unchecked on a regular basis are like laundry. The more days I put it off, the more I have to deal with, the more it smells, and the more I avoid it. But at some point, unless I am into wearing dirty, stinky clothes, I am going to have to do some cleaning.

Repentance, or change of thinking and actions, is laundry service for our spirits. It feels good and clean! But like laundry, repentance is a process that keeps going. To keep our hearts good and clean, we have to remove the dirt.

My Desires ...

We all have desires! The good news is that God wants to fulfill those desires. He longs to give us the desires of our hearts — at least, the desires he knows will give us abundant lives. Some of our desires could ultimately bring destruction, so he might not answer the way we would like him to. It is like a parent/child relationship. We want to give our kids the things they desire, but if we gave them all the things they desired, it would be a disaster. It's the same with our relationship with God. He longs to give us what we desire, but he also knows what will cause disaster in our lives!

Suggestions ...

I really love this part because it gets me thinking of ways to do things differently or better. It gives me a chance to go beyond where I am and challenges me to take action to make my life the fullest it can be for that day.

Let's run this race ... together.

Day #1:
TEMPTATION

The Sense of Humor Spot:
> I typically avoid temptation, except when I can't resist it!

WORD

If you fight with temptation like I do, this is for YOU. Deep down, I want to overcome and move on, but the door of temptation keeps knocking, and I find myself answering the door.

As I read the story about Jesus being tempted in the desert, I am encouraged to know there is a style or pattern, if you will, for us to use to combat temptations daily when they come to us. Temptations will come! I see how important *words* are through this temptation Jesus faced in the desert.

Jesus didn't pull out a phone and call someone for help. He didn't run to a friend, a family member, a drink, the tube, the Internet, a drug, a prescription, or a weapon. He didn't act out in anger, hide, or run. No, He spoke the s-Word. When he was tempted, he answered, "It is written. It is written. It is written."

Jesus had been fasting for 40 days and was physically weak when the tempter, Satan, came to tempt him in the desert. Satan does that to us. He is clever and knows just when to push our buttons, like when we are tired, hungry, our bank account is empty, our marriage is rocky, we are on the verge of snapping, or if we are walking into a stressful situation. He knows just how to tempt us to put God to the test.

He also likes to offer us shortcuts to life that offer temporary victory, but lead to everlasting defeat, if we aren't aware and walking in God's will for our lives. Let's get into God's will for our lives together.

Come with me to Matthew 4:1-11

Then Jesus was led by the Spirit into the desert to be tempted by the devil. After fasting forty days and forty nights, he was hungry. What kind of temptation comes to me when I am hungry or have other physical desires? Maybe I lose my temper; I get moody; I get sideways with my kids or my husband. You don't wanna be around momma when it's feeding time. Or maybe I fall into a relationship that is not one I need to be in, but I am searching for that someone or feeling to fill my emotional void. *The tempter came to him and said, "If you are the Son of God, tell these stones to become bread."* Is there something you *could* do in your power, but know it's against what your conscience is telling you to do? Satan was trying to get Jesus to "prove himself." He said, "If you are the Son of God." I have to know who I am and not feel I must prove myself to anyone but GOD. *Jesus answered, "It is written: 'Man does not live on bread alone, but on every word that comes from the mouth of God.'"* This is very interesting to me because food is very interesting to me — like really interesting to me, as it was to Eve. Food and the things we put in our mouth seem to be one of the first weapons Satan uses to destroy us.

As it is in our physical bodies, we need some healthy whole food — and on a regular basis. So it is in our spirits. We *live* life abundantly by feeding our spirits on every healthy whole *word* that comes from the mouth of God. Jesus answered with the foundation of truth he had. He quoted scripture. He quoted a principle from the s-Word of God which then guided his decisions.

I need *principle scriptures* in my heart, mind, and spirit. I get these by studying the Word and being led by the Spirit of God. If I eat only whole healthy food, I won't have room for the junk food. That is the same in our spirits. We have to feast on truth, rather than go through famine in our spirits by watching, listening, speaking, and reading junk. This is a process! It takes time to change our thinking from junk to TRUTH.

Then the devil took him to the holy city and had him stand on the highest point of the temple. In the "holy city" of our lives God will not change *his* principles, he will not be tested. *"If you are the Son of God,"* he said, *"throw yourself down. For it is written: 'He will command his angels concerning you, and they will lift you up in their hands, so that you will not strike your foot against a stone.'"* See how that dirty devil will even use the word of God (he said, "For it is written") and twist it just a touch to allow just a little bit of doubt to creep in? I have to know what God's word says so that I will know when the enemy is twisting ever-so slightly to get me to do things for immediate gratification, instead of waiting on God to fulfill my needs. There are no shortcuts to reach a worthy goal — God's plan calls for the cross before the crown. We must die to our flesh to see God's glory.

Jesus answered him, "It is also written: 'Do not put the Lord your God to the test. Again, the devil took him to a very high mountain and showed him all the kingdoms of the world and their splendor. "All this I will give you," he said, *"if you will bow down and worship me."* I have been taken to the mountain tops and have been tempted with fancy, nice, beautiful things of this world, but those things and positions, compromised my belief, myself, my conscience, and my God. How about you? Unfortunately, I gave in many times to those temptations only to find myself in a valley. *Jesus said to him, "Away from me, Satan! For it is written: 'Worship the Lord your God, and serve him only.'"* *Then the devil left him, and angels came and attended him.* I have learned that the devil will leave me when I speak the written word of God. My friend, the devil will leave you alone when you speak truth because darkness cannot hide in light; therefore, when you and I speak the written word, the devil has to flee.

What I Learned:

There are three areas in which human beings are especially vulnerable to when it comes to temptations. The first is our physical needs and desires. The second is people who refuse to take God's presence in faith, but demand God to "prove Himself." The third temptation is to take shortcuts in life and abandon the will of God for our lives.

In which one of these areas do you need to get a word to combat those temptations that come your way? Here are three ways to overcome temptations:

#1. Seek out scriptures that declare victory over your temptations, like Jesus did. Fight like Jesus!

#2. Trust God and have faith in God's word. Put your faith into action.

#3. Pray and fast (the act or practice of abstaining from food or other pleasure in order to put focus on the Lord) from those things that tempt you.

Your turn in the Word:

"Watch and _____ so that you will not fall into _____. The spirit is willing, but the body is _____ " (Matthew 26:41).

Joy's example: *This tells me that I need to watch and pray in order to avoid temptation.*

_____

_____

_____

Thinking of Others ...

Thank you, LORD! Thank you for knowing exactly which friend needs deliverance from temptations right now, today. Set them free from thinking "they can do it" and let them know through YOU they can be overcomers. God, let us see that Jesus' only resource was scripture. He understood that God's principles will never change. Jesus believed your word, spoke it, and overcame the enemy. I pray for my family and friends that they would believe your word, speak your word, and see the freedom that comes from that process.

Joy's example: *God, help me to teach Emily and Remi to use your word to fight temptations that will come their way.*

_____

_____

_____

_____

Repentance ...

Father, I pour out TODAY what I need to change, and pour in TODAY what I need to become more like You. I understand true freedom comes from taking responsibility for my decisions, actions, and choices. I know I have to be real with you, God, and write down the choices I am making that I don't want to make, but I do anyway. I need to decide how I am going to CHANGE those choices to choices that will glorify YOU.

Joy's example: *I seek out truth from others rather than God. I am going to spend more focused time with God and get His truth.*

_____

_____

_____

_____

My desires ...

God, my desire is to be "tempted" by YOU and YOUR ways. God I want to overcome any temptation that takes me away from my TRUE relationships with you and others. I know that my temptations keep me away from having deep relationships with you and others.

Joy's example: *I want to overcome the same pattern of temptations I have dealt with most of my life.*

_____

_____

_____

_____

What do my temptations look like? How can I change those temptations I struggle with? Do I have a friend or family member who is in a deep, real relationship with the Lord that I trust and can go to for prayer and encouragement? GO!

Listen, they struggle, too. We all do! We are better together! There is one *true counselor* — the s-Word of God!

Day #2:
ASK, SEEK, KNOCK

The Sense of Humor Spot:

A father and son went fishing one day. After a couple hours out in the boat, the boy suddenly became curious about their surroundings. He asked his father, "How does this boat float?"

The father thought for a moment, then replied, "Don't rightly know, son."

The boy returned to his contemplation, then turned back to his father, "How do fish breathe underwater?"

Once again, the father replied, "Don't rightly know, son."

A little later, the boy asked his father, "Why is the sky blue?"
Again, the father replied. "Don't rightly know, son."
Worried he was going to annoy his father, he says, "Dad, do you mind my asking you all of these questions?"
"Of course not, Son. If you don't ask questions, you'll never learn anything!"

Word

Ask — to pray, to desire, crave, make supplication, require, long for
Seek — to worship God, to seek in order to find, to seek in order to find by thinking or meditating, to desire, to exert oneself to do or effect something, make an effort, inquire, search for something hidden, to learn, understand
Knock — to communicate; to knock smartly or lightly as to make a noise

Come with me to Matthew 7:7-14

Ask and it will be given to you; God already knows your requests, but like us, we want to be asked, not just expected to give. Go to God and ask him for what is on your heart, and it will be given to you. When our kids ask us for something, we want to give it to them (most of the time). Why? Because we love them and long to fulfill their needs. But there are times we may not give our children what they ask for because we know the timing may not be right, like giving a car to a 12-year-old. That 12-year-old couldn't handle it. It's not the right time. The same is true for us. God is sovereign and knows everything. If he gives us something or does not give it to us, it's because he knows the "big picture."

Seek and you will find; Find what? You discover God by searching the scriptures and BS-ing (studying the Bible), and then looking around in your day for him. I have found that when I am looking for God, I see him in most situations if I am seeking him. Be a seeker by asking questions of people who are truly believing in the King of Kings. My friend, no one can do this for you. Oh, the reward for being a seeker!

Knock and the door will be opened to you. When was the last time you stood at someone's front door and expected them to answer without you knocking? Knock; let him know you want to come into his presence by inviting him into your everyday life.

For everyone who asks receives; Did you get that? His promise is that "everyone who asks receives." Get ready to receive God's will. Remember, God is sovereign. He will only answer your prayers in his way, which is the best way, not our way. Therefore, if you seek scriptures and have an ongoing, conversational relationship with God, you begin to know who he is. *he who seeks finds;* Did you really get that, too? He who seeks finds. You will find God's truth for your situation. For example, when you lose something, then you start seeking to find it; and when you find it, you are so thankful, excited, and glad you put the effort in to find it. When I find a word that I know God is speaking to me, I get so excited, because I have found something that I was looking for: a word of truth for me. God is very personal.

We have two girls, and they are very different in their personalities. We have learned that we all understand one another better when we meet our girls on their individual levels and take their individual personalities into consideration. God will speak to you differently than he speaks to anyone else.

and to him who knocks, the door will be opened. When is the last time you stood outside someone's door knowing they were there, but they didn't answer? Or you thought they would never answer because it took them so long to open up the door? God is not like that. He promises that if you knock on his door he will let you in. But God is not a butler; he answers when he knows you will honor him. **Which of you, if his son asks for bread, will give him a stone?** If my kids asked for some food, and I just gave them a bowl of rocks, they would think I "lost my rocks," if you know what I mean. God wants to give you what you ask, according to his will and his word. *Or if he asks for a fish, will give him a snake?* That would be some prank — to hand my kids a snake instead of a fish. Of course fish is something my kids never ask for! I keep trying to convince them that fish tastes good, but I have had no breakthrough yet!

If you, then, though you are evil, know how to give good gifts to your children, how much more will your Father in heaven give good gifts to those who ask him! So in everything, (yep, everything!) *do to others what you would have them do to you,* If you want to be gossiped about, gossip. If you want to be hated, hate. If you want to be loved, show love. If you want respect, give respect. *for this sums up the Law and the Prophets.* It is a law, a principle; therefore, it does not change. God does not change. Ask, seek, and knock, and who God is and what his promises are will be revealed to YOU.

What I learned:

Ask: God wants to have a relationship with you. Just as when our kids ask us for everything from comfort, food, shelter, love, forgiveness, hope, and so much more, we give it to them because they ask. "Mom, can I have something to eat (provision)? Dad, I need help with this problem (comfort/guidance). I am scared and don't know what to do about this situation (wisdom)." Ask, my friend. He is waiting on you. You are not waiting on him. He will tell you, fill you, and comfort you. He will!

Seek: Dive into the scriptures. Look for him in daily life through actions of others. When you see someone give love, that love is God in them. We are his hands and feet. You must get knowledge. Look in the verse below and see what happens when we choose not to (refuse to) seek knowledge of who God is. Hosea 4:6 says, "My people are destroyed from lack of knowledge. 'Because you have rejected knowledge, I also reject you as my priests; because you have ignored the law of your God, I also will ignore your children.'"

Knock: We have to go to the door and knock. How will we know who God is if we don't knock on his door and go inside his home? You can learn so much from being inside a person's home. Just like us, God's dwelling place is in his word and in our hearts. We have to learn his word, his ways, his thoughts. We must get the word in us and then begin to speak like he speaks, so he will live in us and through us.

Your turn in the Word:

"But _____ first his kingdom and his righteousness, and all these things will be _____ to you as well" (Matthew 6:33).

_____

_____

_____

Thinking of Others ...

Light of the world, you came down into darkness for us. You came and humbled yourself to look, feel, live, and breathe like us. You taught us while you were here how to ask, seek, and knock. Help my family, my friends, and the person reading this to want to seek out your light in this dark world.

_____

_____

Repentance ...

God, forgive me for going to people, places, or things to ask, seek, and knock instead of you. Forgive me for not seeking you first. Father, I have been so foolish to not seek you out like a precious jewel, but instead I have sought out excuses for wanting to do things my way. Jesus, you came to set me free. I choose to change my ways for your ways.

_____

_____

_____

My Desires ...

My Refiner, how I long to seek you instead of this world's answers. I desire to communicate with you. I am knocking at your door, Father, and I know you are on the other side waiting to open it for me and teach me all of your ways. Thank you for your promises of freedom!

_____

_____

_____

When is the last time I really asked God something and just talked to him? (Notice, I did not merely ask when was the last time you asked for some "thing.")

Have you ever searched for God by seeking him out through reading scriptures, asking questions, and just looking for him in everyday life? Have you ever thought what it would be like to just knock on your Creator's door?

Let's try it right now! I'll help you start ...

God, I am here at your door. I would like to invite you into my life, and I would like to know, truly know, you. I believe you sent your son to die for me. Please forgive me of my sins and allow me to become one with you. I ask this in your name. Amen!

Get ready my friend, you are a new creation! It's PARTY time!! I am shaking my bootie and clapping my hands for YOU!

Day #3:
THE SWORD

The Sense of Humor Spot:

TEACHER: Now, John, tell me frankly, do you say prayers before eating?

JOHN: No sir, I don't have to, my mom is a good cook.

WORD

Oh my sista' and bro', please, hear this word. I have been seeking God for many years. As I get this in my daily life, I have victory. Please don't

take as long as I have to really believe God and this truth: I now believe the helmet of salvation is the covering of our minds.

The battle always begins in the mind. Our behavior is a result of our thinking. This is why it so important to be mindful of whom and what we are surrounding our lives. Put on the helmet of salvation to protect your mind and thoughts. Then you will have the power to slice through any place of addiction, unbelief, pride, deception, rejection, guilt, loss, depression, sexual stronghold, insecurity, financial difficulties, feeling of being unloved, or loss of respect.

All of these areas are covered, healed, and set free by the sword — the sword of the Spirit, which is the word of God. That's right, nothing this world can offer you will change any of those things or places in your life like the sword of the Spirit, the word of God.

If you were fighting for your child's life (I tend to fight for others more than myself, so this helps me to look at it like this), and the only weapon you had to choose from was a drink, a cute leopard print shirt, or a sword, which would you pick up? A sword, right? I know I would. You see, we pick up so much other "stuff" to try to fight the battle. Man, why has it taken me so long to just speak the word of God, instead of trying all the world has offered me to "help" me overcome my battles?

Of course, with prayer, faith, and action, we will have victory. Remember how we said earlier that our behavior is a result of our thinking? When is the last time an s-Word came to your mind about a problem you were having? When you have a situation, the first place to always run to is the Bible, our sword. Even if you don't know how to look up scriptures that are specifically for your situation, there are so many resources to help you find them. But you have to want to win the battle!

Come with me to Ephesians 6:17

Take or understand, possess, receive ... take it, my friend. Want it; go get it! *the helmet* This protects your head or mind. Satan knows if he can get you thinking sin, you will sin; therefore, that is why it is so important to take captive every thought. In other words, be a slave to thinking God's thoughts, not the enemy's thoughts or ways. You will be a slave to something ... a job, a drug, a person, or whatever. Choose what is better. Be a slave for Christ. Since the beginning of man, Satan has attacked the mind. He is after your thinking. *of salvation* (deliverance from the power and penalty of sin) *and the Sword* I think God is so purposeful in his written

Word that he included "word" in the word "sword." It's our s-Word. Yes, it will turn heads and hearts. It is our "Superman." Jesus is the Word. The Word was God and the Word was with God. Our protection comes from the word. You create a sword to fight the enemy with when you use the word of God by speaking it and believing it. *of the Spirit* (God), *which is the word of God* Our swords look and sound like words. Speak and read your weapon into reality. If what you say lines up with the word, then you have created a s-Word.

What I Learned:

Take the helmet of salvation — protect your mind.

Take the s-Word of the Spirit — understand, possess, and receive the written Words of God and spoken Words that God speaks to your heart.

Take the Word of God — No one can do this for you. You choose the words you speak. Choose life words.

Your turn in the Word:

"The _____ of sinful man is death, but the _____ controlled by the Spirit is life and peace ..." (Romans 8:6).

_____

_____

_____

Thinking of Others ...

Lord, may the mediations of our hearts and the words of our mouths be pleasing to you, so that we may be a light for all those we are praying over today. Father, let our minds be controlled by the Spirit and free us from the sinful mindsets that so easily take us away from You.

_____

_____

_____

My Desires ...

God, let me have a hunger for your truth, to want to know the scriptures for myself and not expect others or things to set me free when only your sword can slice the heart of sin out of my life.

_____

Draw a sword with your own favorite scriptures. Here is what mine looks like:

ISAIAH 40:31 PSALMS 19:14

HEBREWS 4:12

MATTHEW 11:28–30

ROMANS 12:2

PSALMS 119:105

JOHN 16:22

1 PETER 5:6-7

JOHN 3:12

EPHESIANS

PSALMS 63:1–11

JOHN 1:1 PSALMS

Day #4:
THE O-WORD: obeDIEnce

The Sense of Humor Spot:

Man to dog trainer: "Every time a bell rings, my dog goes into the corner."

Dog trainer: "That's OK; he is a boxer."

WORD

The o-word is the one word I struggle with most. As you see, "I die" is in the center of the word obeDIEnce. No one wants to talk about death,

except maybe morticians. Obedience demands action, and that kind of action is usually something we resist! Obedience is a call to stop what you think you want to do and to do what is right. Let's take my children, for example. I may keep telling them the right thing to do, and they disobey over and over again. It is so clear to me. If they would just obey, it would open the door for me to give them what I really want to give them, which is the desires of their heart.

But, that is the problem with me and my obedience — I've got to get my bootie (the b-word at the beginning of this sentence) out of the way and start obeying exactly what God is telling me to do, either through my study of scripture ("Logos" word — this is for you BS-ers who have already been BS-ing and want some more meat to chew on) or through what he speaks to me in my conscience or Spirit ("Rhema" word ... again this for those BS-ers who want to go deeper).

Come with me to John 15:9-12

As the Father has loved me, so have I loved you Jesus walked a fruitful life. He did everything his Father asked. He even died on the cross for us. Imagine how hard it was for him to be that obedient and to give up his whole life. Yet it wasn't in vain. We live. He lives eternally now in heaven, on the earth, and in us. Oh, Jesus, thank you for your obedience. You laid down everything for me and my friends. *Now remain in my love.* True love is not just saying, "I love you." True love is doing what pleases God. Like my kids, when they obey me — I know they really love me because true love reveals itself through actions.

If You get to choose to obey. I choose to obey because I want to show God I love him and I am his child. *you obey my commands, you will remain in my love* (His love is his commands, his promises, and his words), *just as I have obeyed my Father's commands and remain* (eternally) *in His love. I have told you this so that your joy* What happens when our kids obey us? It brings us joy! We know their obedience will give them life. When they disobey, it gets them in trouble or could cause pain, or even death. *may be in you and that your joy may be complete.* My rest, in other words. You find rest when you do what he asks of you. *My command is this: Love* Love is doing! *each other as I have loved you.* He gave his whole life for us. Greater love has no one than this, that he lay down his life for his friends. I find I am happiest when I live my life serving others as God lays it on my heart, which is that Rhema word.

W*hat* I l*ea*rn*e*d:

Jesus gave his whole life for me out of obedience to his father. Just like I want my kids to obey, I know God longs for me to die to my selfish wants and needs and listen to his voice. Just as he has loved me, he asks me to love others through obeying his written words (commands) and obeying the voice in my conscience (my spirit), moment by moment and day by day. It is a process that takes reading and understanding the word, then listening and doing.

Don't get discouraged because this process is ongoing for all of us on this earth. Trust me, we all struggle with obedience and most of us try to escape with partial obedience.

Y*our* t*u*rn *i*n th*e* W*ord*:

"And this is love: that we walk in _____ to his commands. As you have heard from the beginning, his command is that you walk in _____" (II John 1:6).

_____

_____

_____

Thinking of Others ...

Father, I know I struggle with full obedience, and I am thinking my friends, family, and those reading this book may have the same struggle with immediate, full obedience. God, help each one of us to have the desire to choose to listen and obey immediately/fully the Spirit's voice inside us directing us moment by moment down the right path. Help us not to deny your way.

_____

_____

_____

Repentance ...

Gracious God, I am sorry for disobeying you. I realize I cannot rest in simply saying sorry, but I must choose to think differently, change my behavior and my thoughts and acknowledge your principles, patterns, and precepts as my way of life.

_____

_____

_____

My Desires ...

God, I desire to love (obey) you in each moment of this day, and especially right now.

_____

_____

_____

What is hindering me from obeying God fully? What plan of action can I take to help me get into full obedience with God?

I choose life or death! Which choice will lead me to life? Or to death?

Day #5:
LOVE ONE ANOTHER

The Sense of Humor Spot:
> Do you believe in love at first sight? Or do I have to walk by again?

WORD

Love is a word that has so many dimensions. Love is a smile, a hug, an act of service for someone else that goes beyond self: a meal, a word of encouragement, a tear that falls for another being, day in and day out of sacrificing your life for one another, or even a kiss on the cheek of an enemy.

Love reaches places that no other thought or feeling can get to. Love does. Love is an action, that when in full motion, not only changes the person extending it, but also heals the person receiving love. Love always conquers, always wins, and always brings victory. When I look at the word love, I notice that in the letter v there are two lines that come together and connect. The way to loVe is by connecting yourself with someone else. Also, notice how the lines go down to connect to that point. I believe to truly loVe, we must humble ourselves, go down, reach toward that situation or person, and rise up together.

Come with me to John 15:12-13

My command What he directs us to do will benefit us abundantly. is this Listen to His simple command. LOVE A profound tender, affection for another person. I want some of that! one another Love one another, not myself. as I have loved you. He gave everything. He gave his only son to be loved rejected, denied, tortured, and to DIE for you and me to have eternal life. Greater love has no one than this, that he lay down his life for his friends. Everyone wants to do something great and profound, yet it's so simple that we miss it sometimes. That great something requires simply loving another by showing a profound, tender affection to another.

What I Learned:

What I have learned is that my leader, my Jesus, gives me commands to lead me to V-I-C-T-O-R-Y. I feel like cheering that. He gives us instruction to prosper us. He says, "This is the one command I leave with you" — to love.

Why love, God? His answer is, "It covers everything."

Oh, I think about the times I was unlovable to myself (I didn't like myself) and someone would just hug on me, either with their arms, a word, or an action, that revealed love to me. It gave me hope and desire to keep going.

Your turn in the Word:

"This is how we know what _____ is: Jesus Christ laid down his life for us. And we ought to lay down our lives for our brothers" (I John 3:16).

_____

_____

_____

Thinking of Others ...

Again, I John 3:16 "This is how we know what love is: Jesus Christ laid down his life for us." And we ought to lay down our lives for our brothers.

God, who can I lay down a part of my day for — today — and show love by a saying a prayer, making a phone call, speaking a word of encouragement, giving a hug or just a simple smile?

_____

_____

_____

Repentance ...

God, while I was writing this about love, I was unloving to my kids and husband. They definitely did not "feel the love." I know living life in a relationship with you is an ongoing process. Teach me to walk in your love.

_____

_____

_____

My Desires ...

In I John 3:18, it says: "Dear children, let us not love with words or tongue, but with actions and in truth. Lord, my desire is to let my actions be love to others."

_____

_____

_____

Attach a photo or make a list of those you want to show intentional love to — today!

Plan a special surprise for your kids; go to lunch with a friend; watch football with your man!

Love someone today!

Day #6:
MAKE UP MY MIND

The Sense of Humor Spot:

A woman was driving to work when a truck ran a stop sign, hit her car broadside, and knocked her out cold. A passerby pulled her from the wreck and revived her. She began a terrific struggle and had to be tranquilized by the medics.

Later, when she was calm, they asked her why she struggled so.

She explained, "I remember the impact, then nothing. I woke up on a concrete slab in front of a huge, flashing 'Shell' sign, but somebody was standing in front of the 'S'!"

WORD

There is an old Cherokee legend that goes like this: An old Cherokee grandmother is teaching her granddaughter about life. "A fight is going on inside me," she said to the little girl. "It is a terrible fight and it is between two wolves. One is good — she is joy, peace, love, hope, serenity, humility, kindness, goodness, empathy, generosity, truth, compassion, and faith.

"The other is evil," the grandmother continued. "She is full of anger, envy, sorrow, regret, greed, arrogance, self-pity, addictions, guilt, resentment, inferiority, lies, false pride, superiority, and ego. The same fight is going on inside you — and inside every other person, too."

The granddaughter thought about it for a minute with great curiosity and then asked her grandmother, "Which wolf will win?"

The old Cherokee simply replied, "The one you feed."

You see, I have a "set of twins" inside of me, or opposing thoughts and ideas. One wants what is right. I know the voice inside me that is telling me to make the right choice. I also have another voice that is almost louder at times that is telling me to do the total opposite. I know what is right, but I always seem to justify the little "this is no big deal lie." So I do what I want and not what is right. I am so guilty of this — almost daily.

Whether it's with my attitude, my spending, my words, my eating or anything else that I swallow, the way I spend my time, or so many more small ways we overlook those "small things" for instant gratification.

If I could ever just get it in my heart and in my head that God wants to constantly guide me with the "right voice." He knows that if I choose right, I will be so much more: more joyful, more stable, more loving, more truthful, more consistent, more peaceful, more compassionate, much more happy, more of who I was meant to be.

Notice I said, "Who I was meant to be." It is vital to understand each one of us is totally different. I must only measure myself by God's design for me and not look to others for measuring my worth or my value.

Come with me to James 1:2-8

Consider it pure joy, my brothers, whenever you face trials of many kinds I don't know about you, but when I am facing trials, I am not thinking pure joy. This is a great example of why you need to know the s-Word, because it changes your perspective during trials. *because you know that the testing of your faith develops perseverance.* One definition for perseverance: continuance in a state of grace to the end, leading to eternal salvation. *Perseverance must finish its work so that you may be mature and complete, not lacking anything. If any of you lacks wisdom,* Wisdom — knowing what you should do and doing it. *he should ask God,* How do you ask someone for something? That's the way you ask God. Communicate with him, not your friends or your thoughts, but talk to him. *Who gives generously to all without finding fault, and it will be given to him.* It's just like your kids; you give to them generously. He wants to do that for us, but we have to walk in his way. We give to our kids generously when they obey.

But when he asks, he must believe and not doubt, When you ask God for something, you have to know, to believe he can do it. It's just the way it works because he who doubts is like a wave of the sea, blown and tossed by the wind. When you doubt, you look for other ways, people, places, or things to believe in. All these "ways" change. But God never changes. *That man should not think he will receive anything from the Lord; he is a double-minded man, unstable in all he does.* Unfortunately, I can relate with that!

What I Learned:

I have two voices in me, good and evil. I have to choose to feed the good voice of God, by listening and doing what he says. Pray with total belief that God can do what you ask if it is his will.

Your turn in the Word:

"What _____ fights and quarrels among you? Don't they come from our _____ that battle within you?" (James 4:1)

_____

_____

_____

Thinking of Others …

God, help my family, my friends, and me to submit to you. Help us resist the devil, because when we resist the devil by speaking s-Words, he has to flee. Your word says darkness cannot hide in light.

_____

_____

_____

Repentance …

God, I have been double-minded in so many ways. Please purify my heart and my mind in all areas that I am listing below. God, through You I can change and overcome. I choose to change, because that is what true repentance is — change!

_____

_____

_____

My Desires …

I long to have a mind that is set only on you and your ways. I don't want to battle the two wolves. Help me to feed and nurture only the good in my life. I want to mature. I want more of you!

_____

_____

_____

Attach, make a list, or draw a picture of what your two wolves look like. Or what causes you to be double-minded? Which one do you nurture (feed or give in to) more?

How could you begin to feed the "wolf" that will bring you love, joy, peace, patience, kindness, goodness, faithfulness, gentleness, and self-control?

Remember, lack of knowledge is why people perish. If you lack self-control, study the topic of self-control. Read every scripture in the Bible that speaks to this. God will show you how to listen to the "right" voice.

Day #7:
GRACE

The Sense of Humor Spot:

There was a newly married couple arguing over who was going to make the coffee. The wife said, "The Bible says that men should make the coffee.

The husband replied, saying, "No, it does not! Show me."

The wife said, "It says, "HE-BREWS."

Word

Grace is one of the most amazing characteristics of God. It is undeserved favor that is given to us moment by moment. You can't earn it or do anything to gain it. It just is. You receive grace and give it freely. Grace is sufficient to cover a multitude of sins. Grace is like a warm, fuzzy blanket you put over someone who is freezing cold, scared, and needs comfort — a someone who happens to be the last person on earth you would want to put a fuzzy blanket on (like an ex-husband, a backstabbing friend, a kid that just punched your kid). That, my friend, is grace.

Grace is divine favor and spiritual blessing. Divine favor is so evident when it happens to me. It is real, and it is so humbling, because I am the last person who deserves unmerited favor. Have you ever received anything that you knew you didn't deserve?

Come with me to Psalm 86:15 & John 1:17

But you, O Lord, are a compassionate and gracious God, God is your Father, your real dad! He is so understanding. He can't wait for you to talk to him, because he is eager to comfort you! *slow to anger,* It's true. He won't reach back from the front seat of the car and spank ya' the way we parents try to do with our kids! (It's funny how long my arms can extend in my car. Of course, my kids don't think it's too funny.) *abounding in love* He is passionate about you, and he is totally devoted to you. *and faithfulness.* God is totally loyal and true. *For the law* The Ten Commandments are our "boundaries" given to us to protect us from each other and ourselves. *was given through Moses; grace* God knows we live in a fallen, sinful world, and he knew there was no way for us to obey the Ten Commandments without wrapping them with grace. Grace is the goodwill, loving-kindness, and favor exerted by God. Grace influences our souls and turns us to him. Grace keeps us and strengthens us in the Christian faith.

What I learned:

All my shame is covered by God's amazing grace. The only condition is that I take it, receive it, live in it, and believe it. Oh, and one more — give grace freely, abundantly, and fully to others. As he has given to me, I want to give.

Your turn in the Word:

"But he said to me, 'My grace is _____ for you, for my power is made perfect in _____.' Therefore, I will boast all the more gladly about my weaknesses, so that Christ's power may rest on me" (II Corinthians 12:9).

_____

_____

_____

Thinking of Others ...

Grace Giver, you already know how weak we are. You sent your Son for us so that we can know you in a real way. You gave us favor and we don't deserve it, but God help us to reach down and receive it. I ask that you reach into the hearts of those I love and soften them in a way that only you can do.

_____

_____

_____

Repentance ...

Counselor, I cannot be set free until I talk to you honestly about my mistakes, my intentional and non-intentional choices. I choose to write down the areas I need forgiveness in today. I will have more tomorrow, but hopefully less than today, if I completely get real with you, my Counselor.

_____

_____

_____

My Desires...

Christ Jesus, I desire to have a grace-giving countenance that spreads throughout my words and my actions each day. Let the influence of the Holy Spirit operate in me today to give strength to others. Also, allow me to be regenerated through your grace, Father.

_____

_____

_____

Name some instances where you have experienced grace (favor you didn't deserve).

Here are some of mine...

My man!
My healthy, happy kids!
Being forgiven!

Day #8:
REST

The Sense of Humor Spot:
I get it now why they call the bathroom a rest-room. Some brilliant mom figured out the only place in the house (most days) that we can go and rest, oddly enough, is in a 4-by-4-foot cubicle that has no laundry, no dishes, no noise. The only noise or mess is our own. (OK, so we take what we can get!) At times, I think I may have even fallen asleep on my rest-ing spot!

WORD

Rest — I think I have all the sleep-deprived moms' attention. I, like most moms, are like, "Yeah, I'd like a little non-interrupted do-what-I-want-time (without the guilt) like sleeping in, reading a whole book at one time, taking a long bath, or just permission to leave clothes on the floor."

I am not only talking about that kind of rest, but I am talking about resting in the Lord. Resting in the Lord is one of toughest, yet most rewarding blessings that I have gained in studying the s-Word.

Some words that describe rest: comfortable, ease, quiet, stillness, to cease from motion, (be) quiet, set down, lean, to rely, tranquility, freedom from anything that wearies, troubles, or disturbs, a period or interval of inactivity, a support, halt, stop.

When I cease from "doing it all on my own, my way" and begin to trust God, his ways, and his guidance, and take on his character in my life, I come to this place of true rest. I wake up, my feet hit the floor, then the whirlwind of getting my family fed, dressed, out the door, dishes, laundry, doctor visits, driving the mom "taxicab" all day, relationships, finances, shopping, homework, baths, dinner, and on and on. There can be a resting place in the middle of all this! It's called relying on God, calling upon his s-Word to help me find the words, the energy, the wisdom to get it all done with joy, peace, and understanding.

Only through him can I do the impossible. God is so simple. Girl, I sure can complicate things with doing things my way. When I truly trust in his ways, I find this rest that can only be known in a real relationship with him. If I study my s-Word, I know he says he is directing my footsteps. He knows the end from the beginning.

So, Momma now knows all that worry is coming from not trusting in him completely. For instance, I can walk into a place (job interview, a new school, anything that gives me insecurity) where I feel uncomfortable and unsure, and I can call upon God and say, "Lord, I know who I am in you. You control all these situations; you already know the end from the beginning. I will walk in peace of mind, spirit, and body because I trust you, not me, anyone else, or anything else."

Girlfriend, just call on the Almighty. Now let him do the work and completely trust in him. That is rest!

Come with me to Psalm 91:1, Exodus 33:14, & Hebrews 4:6-11

Psalm 91:1 — *He who dwells* (Lives in God by having a relationship with him) *in the shelter of the Most High will rest in the shadow of the Almighty.* Have you ever been in the scorching hot sun and then found a shade tree? That instant relief from the heat is exactly what it feels like when you go to God for shade from the "heat of this world."

Exodus 33:14 — *The LORD replied, "My Presence will go with you, He will always be with you and I will give you rest."* He offers freedom from anything that wearies, troubles, or disturbs me.

Hebrews 4:6-7 — *It still remains that some will enter that rest, and those who formerly had the gospel preached to them did not go in, because of their disobedience.* Obedience is the key to finding the resting place he is offering you! *Therefore* (I love this word, because it means as a result or consequently.) *God again set a certain day* He is so merciful! *calling it Today,* (Yes, it is capitalized, and it means right now, today, this moment.) *when a long time later he spoke through David, as was said before: "Today, if you hear His voice When* you hear the right thing, do it today, do not *harden your hearts."* If you do your own thing, you will not find his rest. *For if Joshua had given them rest, God would not have spoken later about another day.* Thank you, God, for today. *There remains, then, a Sabbath-rest for the people of God; for anyone who enters God's rest* Just doing what God asks you to do, moment by moment, today. *also rests from his own work, just as God did from His. Let us, therefore, make every effort* Just try today to do one thing, just one, even if it seems small to you. Try to listen and do what that right voice is encouraging you to do. *to enter that rest, so that no one will fall by following their example of disobedience.*

What I Learned:

God has given us today to truly find rest for all our worries, troubles, anxious thoughts, and even all our happiness, joy, and freedom. When we listen to his voice, which is the Holy Spirit telling us what is right, moment by moment, and we do what he is counseling us to do, we find ourselves free, whole, hopeful, and resting. We know that by doing what he asks us, we find true rest and peace.

Your turn in the Word:

"Find _____, O my soul, in God alone; my _____ comes from him" (Psalms 62:5).

_____

_____

_____

Thinking of Others ...

Lord, I trust in your perfect resting place. I ask that you give us a desire to do things your way, to understand your word, and to take action and do what you put on our hearts, today. I love people, and I know you love your people ... give my friends listed below rest today!

_____

_____

_____

Repentance ...

Refresher of life, please let me feel your refreshing presence as I reveal to you all my ways that aren't your ways. Lead me all day to be aware of your voice, ask for forgiveness, turn the other way, and stop doing things my way. Let me start right now by confessing, I already want to "do it my way" today. I am already tempted to rebel against your rest. You know my thoughts. I know that through you I can overcome.

(Can anyone else say that living this life is a process?)

_____

My Desires...

You, Lord, are my desire. Write your words on my heart so that I will be in tune with you all day. Give me an eagerness to chase after your will, your way, today!

What can I do or what can I let go of today that he has put on my heart over and over again that will set me free and give me a true rest?

I know my strength is in his s-Word and is multiplied by surrounding myself with other people who live life with him.

Day #9:
REFUGE

The Sense of Humor Spot:

An elderly couple had been experiencing declining memory, so they decided to take a power memory class where one is taught to remember things by association.

A few days after the class, the old man was outside talking with his neighbor about how much the class helped him.

"What was the name of the instructor?" asked the neighbor.

"Oh, ummmm, let's see," the old man pondered. "You know that flower, you know, the one that smells really nice but has those prickly thorns, what's that flower's name?"

"A rose?" asked the neighbor.

"Yes, that's it," replied the old man. He then turned toward his house and shouted, "Hey, Rose, what's the name of the instructor we took the memory class from?"

Word

There is a place; it's a hiding place, a shelter, a place of protection from danger and troubles of this life. There is so much to be said about finding a shelter that can outlast any storm I face in my life. When the storms of life come, where do I run for shelter? Is my shelter a friend, my parents, or a family member? Do I get lost in a job, rely on a drug, or have too many drinks? Do I hide behind my education? Do I turn on the TV so that I can "turn off" the storm? Do I become one with my couch? Do I think that money will solve the real storm? Is food my shelter? Do I get lost in magazines and books? Do I overdo workouts?

Finding the right shelter can protect me from any storm within my heart. When I think of shelter, I think of a place that protects me while I am in it. This is the key. I find shelter when my heart is in line with God's word, and I allow him to protect me emotionally and physically, and I trust him for all my needs. It's when I run to him through talking to him, reading his word, or especially in worshipping, that I find my true protection in a hiding place of total comfort, no matter what the storm. The promises I read in the Bible about the storms in our lives are not promises of fixing the storm or stopping the storm. The promises God gives teach me that he will wrap his "grace wings" around me and protect me through the storm if I run to his shelter and let him be my refuge.

Come with me to Psalm 9:9 & Deut 33:27

Psalm 9:9 — *The Lord is a refuge* Here are some of the Hebrew translations for refuge: a safe, strong, defend, exalt, be excellent, be set on high, lofty, be safe, set up on high, be too strong. *For the oppressed, a strong-hold* is a well-fortified place; a fortress *in times of trouble.*

Deuteronomy 33:27 — *The eternal* (everlasting) *God is your refuge,* He is my safe place to run to, walk to, pray to, laugh with, cry with, to live life with. *and underneath are the everlasting arms.* His arms will never stop holding me. *He will drive out your enemy before you,* He will do the work when I go to him for protection, attention, love — not other things or people. *saying, "Destroy him!"* He will destroy my enemy, even if my enemy is myself. He can destroy anything that is trying to destroy me. No matter how long of a process it is, I will let him work out his perfect will day by day. I am going to keep running back to him.

What I Learned:

There is a safe place called a refuge. He is a strong tower, the too strong tower. I run to his fortress and let him chase away my worries while I rest in his everlasting arms. I even go to him when I want to rejoice, but no one else wants to rejoice with me. He will dance and celebrate with me. He is safe. He never changes.

Your Turn in the Word:

"Every word of God is _____; he is a shield to those who take _____ in him" (Proverbs 30:5).

_____

_____

_____

Thinking of Others ...

Eternal God, you are our refuge. Let everyone I know (and don't know who are reading this book) take shelter in your everlasting arms. Let them know you are safe, strong, and all powerful in the midst of any storm they are in.

Give them a new understanding of who you are to them. If they truly know who you are, they will come to you by praying with you, talking with you, reading with you, all the while trusting that you can hear, see, smell, taste, and touch everything we can, so you understand. You are trustworthy.

_____

_____

_____

Repentance ...

My Refresher, I am sorry that I have run to others to try to find a safe place. I confess that at times I run to things to protect my thoughts. But I know through studying your character that you are my only strong tower. Please forgive me for running from you instead of into your fortress. I will change my way of thinking when storms occur, and I will run to you first!

_____

_____

_____

My Desires ...

My Redeemer, I want to know you in a way that is so deep and so real that my first reaction to a good or bad situation is to run to you. I long to please you by totally trusting you and you only. I understand I have to live this life here on earth, and it is full of good and evil. My desire is to run to good and hate evil.

_____

_____

_____

What does your hiding place look like? Where do you run or who do you run to when you need help?

Look up this scripture: Psalm 91:4-16.

Day #10:
HOLDING UP YOUR ARMS

The Sense of Humor Spot:
An old man goes to the doctor for his yearly physical, his wife tagging along. When the doctor enters the examination room, he tells the old man, "I need a urine sample, a stool sample, and a sperm sample."

The old man, being hard of hearing, looks at his wife and yells, "WHAT? What did he say? What does he want?"

His wife yells back, "He needs your underwear."

WORD

Recently, I called my "soul sista" about a situation I was struggling with, and she said something that will stay in my arsenal to use while we fight the good fight in this process of the Christian journey.

I've got to stop for a second and highlight what I just said. I didn't say "perfect life." I said, "process of the Christian journey." We tend to think because we are Christians that if we aren't perfect, then, well, we can't tell anyone, or we will be rejected by our friends or family. That, my friend, is not how we should live life. Instead, we should live knowing that we are not perfect, that we need Jesus, and we need each other in the Christian journey. We need each other, and we need different "each others" or "a few faith-filled, solid believers," so we can help each other see the full picture of our lives together.

Back to my "soul sista." As I cried out to her, weary with my concerns, she said, "I just want you to know I am holding up your arms." She went on to tell me the story about Moses, Aaron, Hur, and Joshua winning the battle against the Amalekites together. Moses' friends, Aaron and Hur, stood in the gap for him, holding his weary hands up when he could not. And Joshua fought with a sword until the battle was finished, and they had overcome the enemy together.

COME WITH ME TO EXODUS 17:8-15

The Amalekites came and attacked the Israelites at Rephidim. Moses said to Joshua, "Choose some of our men and go out to fight the Amalekites. Tomorrow, I will stand on top of the hill with the staff of God in my hands." So Joshua fought the Amalekites as Moses had ordered, and Moses, Aaron, and Hur went to the top of the hill. As long as Moses held up his hands, the Israelites were winning, but whenever he lowered his hands, the Amalekites were winning. When Moses' hands grew tired, they took a stone and put it under him and he sat on it. Aaron and Hur held his hands up — one on one side, one on the other — so that his hands remained steady till sunset. So Joshua overcame the Amalekite army with the sword.

Let's make this personal. Picture the Amalekites as a struggle or concern that you currently have. Now pretend that you are Moses. (The Israelites would be your family). Joshua, Aaron, and Hur are your friends who are helping you fight your struggle. Your friends help you by praying and by using the s-Word the way that Moses' friends held up his arms. Surround yourself with prayer warriors. Moses' friends stayed with him until V-I-C-T-O-R-Y came. My friends stay with me until my dark cloud is lifted, and I can see the light.

What I Learned:

The very last verse says Joshua overcame the Amalekite army. Obviously, through reading this passage, it wasn't just Joshua who won. He had true friends who helped him overcome. I don't know about you, but I need my girlfriends to hold up my weary, tired self sometimes to get me through some battles.

One of the hardest things for me to do is to reach out to my friends for help. I have so much pride at times. I am scared of rejection. I worry that they won't understand. Those are all very valid reasons not to go to a friend and ask for help, but those are all lies. The enemy doesn't want you to have two or more joined in conversation and prayer. Why? He knows when you have friends in faith, your friends will speak truth into you. They can help you gain understanding, and they can help you identify and cast out anything they hear you saying that does not line up with the s-Word.

Remember, the battle always begins in our minds. You need friends you can trust and who you can share your thoughts with. Trust me on this. There are so many lies you tell yourself, and you don't even know that you are doing it. It is vital to have a circle of believers joined together with you to help you win your wars! Also, your friends need for you to hold up their weary arms in the midst of their battles. Trust is a very valuable treasure. Don't ever lose it or misuse it.

Your Turn in the Word:

"Love must be sincere. Hate what is evil; cling to what is good. Be _____ to one another in brotherly love. Honor one another above _____" (Romans 12:9-10).

_____

_____

_____

Thinking of Others ...

My FRIEND, Jesus, I have friends that need me to hold up their arms. Show me who I can pray for today. Give each one you bring to mind a measure of comfort knowing that I am fighting for them by using the s-Word on their behalf.

_____

_____

_____

Repentance...

Lord Almighty, I have hurt my friends at times with my words or actions. I have not been the shield I should be for them in their battles. God, my jealousy, bitterness, selfishness, and insecurities have gotten the better of me at times. Let my heart be pure before you and before them. Let them know I am a safer friend now, because each day I know you better and become more like you. Those past "things" or "selfish acts" aren't who I am today. Don't let my words or actions ever hinder my friends from coming to me for shelter and comfort; and let me be the friend that holds their arms up when they are weary.

_____

_____

_____

My Desires ...

Savior, keep me so in tune with you that I can hear your voice and speak truth into the battles of everyday life. I long to know your word so well that it just flows off my tongue and creates LIFE in the midst of every conversation, every action, and every relationship.

_____

_____

_____

What is a word of truth that I can speak into a family member's or a friend's life right now?

(One of my personal favorites is Proverbs 3:5-6, "Trust in the Lord with all your heart and lean not on your own understanding. In all your ways acknowledge him, and he will make your paths straight.")

How can I hold the arms of a loved one up while they are weary right now?

Day #11:
HIDDEN IN MY HEART

The Sense of Humor Spot:

A patient needed a brain transplant, and the doctor told the family, "Brains are very expensive, and you will have to pay the costs yourselves."

"Well, how much does a brain cost?" asked the relatives.

"For a male brain, $500,000. For a female brain, $200,000," replied the doctor.

Some of the younger male relatives tried to look shocked, but all the men nodded because they thought they understood. But the patient's daughter was unsatisfied and asked, "Why the difference in price between male brains and female brains?"

"Standard pricing practice," said the doctor. "Women's brains have to be marked down because they've actually been used."

WORD

There is something so fascinating about a mystery. It arouses curiosity. One of the greatest known, but unknown, mysteries that I want to find the answer to is: How do I stop doing what is wrong (sinning) and become free from my bondage? How do I overcome the brownie on my counter?

There is no real mystery in how to stop. The answer is clear: just stop. But my flesh and my desires get in the way of just stopping. Besides, that brownie is looking too right, and it would be so wrong to leave it looking so right. OK, so there are bigger things we struggle with than a brownie (It's when it gets to be the two to five brownies that the struggle begins), but that is why I need to go on a treasure hunt in my heart every once in a while. I need to go find what I truly treasure.

When I want to hide something, where do I go to put it? In a secret place, right? A place that is rare, special, and only I know about it. There is a mystery in my secret place, my heart, which is longing to be unveiled through the word of God. In order to solve the mystery of misery and find the treasure of freedom, I have to hide the s-Word in my heart.

The mystery of my misery is written in God's word, the Bible, and in my heart. God is my Creator. He designed me and knew that I would have this desire to want to do wrong things because of the sinful nature I was born with. He knew that in order for me to overcome, I would have to have an understanding of his word. I have to speak his word, read his word, believe his word, study his word, obey his commands, and hide his word in my heart every day.

As I do these things, my heart and my mind begin to understand truth. Those desires that bring misery to me become less of an issue as the goodness of God fills my heart. He becomes greater, and I become less. Becoming less doesn't sound like a good thing, does it? But when God is greater, my life becomes easier, and it becomes what it was meant to be. I begin to enjoy life where I am, no matter where that is. If the condition of my heart is right, then everything else in my life will begin to line up with the abundant life God promises me in his s-Word.

Come with me to Psalms 119:11

Thy word These are God's promises, principles and precepts that I find in the Bible and in my heart. *have I hid* When I hide something, I do so by covering it and protecting it. *in my heart,* The heart is my will, my intellect, and my mind. *that I might not sin against thee* (KJV).

What I learned:

So the mystery of my misery is solved when I read, listen, obey, pray, study, and understand God's word. His word gives me the desire and the will to do what is right moment by moment. If I don't know or understand God's word and his ways, then how can I stop the bleeding of sin? I can't! The only way to true freedom is by having a relationship with God, moment by moment, day by day.

Your turn in the Word:

"For where your _____ is, there your _____ will be also" (Matthew 6:21).

_____

_____

Thinking of Others ...

My Guide, thank you for giving my friends the desire to find your words and hide them in their hearts so that they will be strong enough to overcome sin and have an abundant life through you. Thank you for being so clear in your word on how to be an overcomer in this world. You gave us your Son to set us free and to give us grace. Help us to be doers of your word!

_____

_____

_____

Repentance ...

Love of my life, God, I have hidden so many things of this world in my heart. They have hindered the treasures you want to place in my heart through your word. I cry out for your mercy all the days of my life. Forgive me for filling my heart with misery instead of your mysteries.

_____

_____

_____

My Desires ...

Provider of true treasures, I want to be so curious of who you are that I seek you out like I would "the perfect dress/house/husband/friend" (I mean that out of respect). But give me the desire to want to seek you, not the things of this earth. I want to have your word written so deeply in my heart that when others hear me or see me, I sound and look like your treasure map.

_____

_____

_____

What do you hide in your heart? What do you treasure? Find one s-Word that you can hide in your heart today!

Day #12:
COUNSELOR

The Sense of Humor Spot:

From a Mother (Who Might Just Be a Redneck), With Love

Dear Child,

I am writing this slow because I know that you can't read fast.

We don't live where we did when you left home. Your dad read in the paper that most accidents happen within 20 miles from your home, so we moved.

I won't be able to send you the address, as the last family that lived here took the house numbers when they left so that they wouldn't have to change their address.

This place is real nice. It even has a washing machine. I'm not sure if it works too well, though. Last week I put a load in, pulled the chain and haven't seen them since.

The weather isn't too bad here. It only rained twice last week. The first time it rained for three days and the second time for four days. The coat you wanted me to send you, your Uncle Steve said it would be a little too heavy to send in the mail with the buttons on, so we cut them off and put them in the pockets.

We got another bill from the funeral home. They said if we don't make the last payment on Grandma's grave, up she comes. John locked his keys in the car yesterday. We were worried because it took him two hours to get me and Shelby out.

Your sister had a baby this morning, but I haven't found out what it is yet, so I don't know if you're an aunt or an uncle. If the baby is a girl, your sister is going to name it after me; she's going to call it Mom.

Uncle Pete fell in a whiskey vat last week. Some man tried to pull him out, but he fought them off and drowned. We had him cremated, and he burned for three days.

Three of your friends went off a bridge in a pick-up truck. Ralph was driving. He rolled down the window and swam to safety. Your two friends were in the back. They drowned because they couldn't get the tail-gate down.

There isn't much more news at this time. Nothing much has happened.

Love, Mom

P.S. I was going to send you some money, but the envelope was already sealed.

WORD

There have been times that I have met with a counselor or friend for help or advice. I totally think it is a good thing to gain insight from another person who has similar beliefs and who understands biblical principles. I knew going into it that there would never be enough time in that hour for the counselor to know everything that has happened in my whole life. That particular person could not even begin to know all that I have been through, the roads I have traveled, the victories, the defeats, all the baggage I have picked up, the joys I have experienced, the things I have left undone, and the people who have shaped my life. Yes, I may feel good for a day after seeing a counselor, but then life happens again, and I need more direction and advice. Sometimes the counselor's next appointment isn't available for another month, or my friend is too busy.

I am a restless girl. I like to control, fix, cure, handle ... always have to be doing something because if I don't do something, then who will? How would you like to have a counselor with you all day? A counselor comes alongside you, gives direction, and helps guides you, right? He or she helps you make right choices, shows you why you should or shouldn't do something, and gives you insight as each moment of the day passes. God is that counselor. You don't have to set an appointment or drive anywhere to see this Counselor.

Girlfriends, hold on to your up-do's, because when I came to the understanding of who "the counselor" is, my life went from an uptight up-do that was held together with a stress bobby pin to letting loose, hair-blowing-in-the-wind daily living. Don't get me wrong, I can have a bad day or two, but it's when I have more than a few bad days in a row, and it becomes a bad life that I realize my desperate need for my Counselor. I have come to the conclusion that if I don't get counsel from him daily, those one or two bad days can turn into a bad season of life — and quick!

Come with me to John 14:25-27

All this I have spoken while still with you. But the Counselor, God is constantly counseling me; it's just that sometimes I don't want to do what the Counselor is advising me to do. So I avoid listening to the voice that is telling me the right way to go. *the Holy Spirit,* Letting the Holy Spirit live in my everyday life, moment by moment, is the key to victory in this life. *whom the father will send in my name, will teach you all things and will remind you of everything I have said to you.* I don't even have to know every scripture inside out to have God counsel me. I just have to be willing to listen and obey his counsel, his small, still voice. *Peace* This peace is a rest, a quietness, a true prosperity. *I leave with you; my peace I give you.* His peace is a gift! Unwrap his gift of peace! *I do not give to you as the world gives.* This world seems to thrive on stress, but I'm taking two of the s's out of that word and doing life God's way through rest. *Do not let your hearts be troubled.* I have to remind myself not to be anxious or worry, but to completely trust God's leading. *and do not be afraid.* I have to ask myself, "Why in the world do I think he would tell us not to be afraid?" I believe it is because he knows what fear does to the human body. It causes doubt, anger, panic, dread, and fills us with apprehension. Besides, he has overcome the world. I am suiting up to go on his team. He has already overcome the world!

What I learned:

God's way is not man's way. I have to understand that principle. When Jesus gave up his life for us on that old rugged cross, God sent the Holy Spirit to dwell in us. He counsels us all day, every day through his written word (the logos) and the spoken word of God (the rhema). The logos, or the written word, is alive, just as the rhema is.

You see, if I or someone I know says they "got a word from God," then it must line up with his written word as well. God speaks to us in our situations. If, only if, we can take action in faith on what he is telling us each day, moment by moment, we will have that peace, his special peace, that the world cannot give.

It's not through a counselor, a surgeon, a dollar bill, a pill, a workout, a friend, a job, an education. Nothing can give you peace like obeying and listening to the counselor: your Counselor, the Holy Spirit. Although God has given us all those great things, wonderful people, and endless educations in our lives to be used for his glory, those things and people are not meant to replace or fill places that only God, our Counselor, fills. He is complete truth!

Your turn in the Word:

"If you _____ me (who?_____) you will obey what I command. And I will ask the _____, and he will give you another _____ to be with you forever — the _____of _____. The world cannot accept him, because it neither _____ him nor knows him. But you know him, for he lives with you and will be in you. I will not _____ you as orphans; I will come to you" (John 14:15-18).

_____

_____

_____

Thinking of Others ...

Spirit of truth, I come to you, seeking out your comfort for my friends. God, let them have an ear to hear and a heart to listen. Give them a willingness to obey your voice. Counsel them right now in their individual situations.

_____

_____

_____

Repentance ...

God, your glory has been squashed by me. Father, I lose myself every time I neglect to listen to your ways, your commands, and your guidance. Father, forgive me for doing this life the world's way and not your way.

_____

_____

_____

Desires ...

I long to know you, my Counselor, in a way that is real and so immediate that as I read scriptures I hear your voice of truth. I want to recognize it and obey you with great joy and enthusiasm because I know your ways are so much better than mine can ever be.

_____

_____

_____

God speaks to me through people, animals, books, you name it. I can see God in them. (The key to that is seeking and looking for God. God's ways are truth; they line up with his word — the Bible — and they are not man's ways.)

How do you see God? How do you know you've had a real experience with God? Take a minute to write it down!

Day #13:
EDIFY

The Sense of Humor Spot:
For your kids or friends who like simple humor:
Europe: what the umpire says when it's your turn to bat.

WORD

Edify means to build up or increase in faith. I don't know about you, but when someone comes into my life who builds me up or causes my faith to increase, I just want to dance and sing. It just gets me through a day of stinkin' thinkin'.

Sometimes (most of the time) it is easier to tear something (or someone) down than to build that thing or someone up. The reason for that is because when you are building, let's say a house for instance, you are not sure what it's going to look like. You know what you want it to look like, but it takes a lot of work and effort to build a house. You have to decide where, when, how, who, how much, why, and so forth.

Think how much easier it is to tear down a house that you already see. That's a no-brainer. Easy, right? Just get the ball and chain and start swinging. The same effort goes into our relationships. I know in my heart when I say things that are critical, I am "removing" or "destroying" a piece of my friend. I understand how bad my flesh can be and especially my tongue. No wonder it is the strongest muscle in the body. It can totally tear a person down with one good tongue-lashing. I never walk away from saying something negative about someone and feel good about myself afterwards. It really hurts me in the end.

Listen, this book is about grace. Are we going to be perfect? No! But when we are in conversation and it begins to go south with words that are tearing another down, it's time to push that self-control, stop button.

On the other hand, I do know how good it feels to edify others. It's like honey in my mouth, and when I open my mouth to edify another, it is sweet to the tongue. You may not taste the true sweetness of what you are speaking over someone immediately, but sooner or later, your edification will build someone up, and you will see a beautiful home being built from the effort of your labor. Saying faith words is tough because faith is something you cannot see.

For instance, I may have a friend who is going through a difficult time, yet I know she can get through it, because if she wants to, she will overcome. As I begin to tell her how I can see her in a year from now being the happiest she has ever been, she begins to feel hope. Do we see that today? No, but those words of edification gave her hope. When you put hope and faith together, then add some edification along with action. You're on your way to building up a beautiful friend.

Come with me to Ephesians 4:29

Do not let any unwholesome false, untrustworthy, untrue *talk* imparting or interchanging thoughts, opinions, or information by speech, writing, or signs *come out of your mouths, but only what is helpful* good, loving, grace-filled *for building others up according to their needs,* Each one of us has a deep desire and need to hear words that are positive about ourselves that build us up and give us that "high-five" feeling. *that it may benefit those who listen.*

What I learned:

It's easier (it seems) to tear something or someone down. Edifying takes grace. Edification builds others up by ministering to their hearts. I am challenging myself today to only choose words that edify others and give grace. Even though I don't see the beautiful person right now, through my words and God's grace, the person I edify will be built into a fortress.

Your turn in the Word:

"Each of us should please his neighbor for his good, to _____him up" (Romans 15:2).

_____

_____

_____

Thinking of Others ...

Strong Tower, refuge in the storm, let me be a builder of strong lives through my words. May your divine blueprint inspire me to speak encouragement, especially over my friends and family members. Show me where they need to be edified and give me the heart to truly minister with grace to their hearts.

_____

_____

_____

Repentance ...

Oh Lord, you know how miserably I have failed in this area. I have spoken partial truths to make myself look better and, in turn, tear someone else down. Father, forgive me for being so careless with others and my words.

_____

_____

_____

My Desires ...

God of Grace, I desire to carry your grace in my actions and in my words on a daily, moment by moment basis. I want to be a craftsman in your handiwork of building up lives in your truth so that they may shine like bright stars in the night.

_____

_____

_____

Whom can you intentionally think about right now who needs to hear a word of encouragement, a true word to help them see that they are precious, they are special, and they are loved?

You would be surprised to know how much people constantly tear themselves down with their thoughts. That is the enemy's best weapon — getting us to think thoughts that destroy us. That is why real relationships are so vital! Celebrate one another through words that edify and build each other up!

Day #14:
A WARM MEAL

The Sense of Humor Spot:
Do cannibals get hungry one hour after eating someone on the Atkins diet?

WORD

Recently, it was both my daughter's and my husband's birthdays. With family coming over that evening for dinner, I had rushed through the day gathering gifts, getting the house cleaned, happily fulfilling my duty as my kid's personal taxi service, etc. All that to say, I forgot to eat. That was a miracle within itself. My angelic mother-in-law brought her famous roast, black-eyed peas, creamed corn, mac and cheese, and my husband's favorite chocolate cake with seven-minute icing for dinner.

Finally, we sat down, took in the aroma and warmth of this home cooked, wonderful creation of a meal. As we were eating, I began to feel warmth in my tummy. I felt comfort. I felt this overwhelming wholeness and fulfillment that was something that I hadn't felt in a while. I am always rushing through the day, eating snacks here and there, but nothing satisfying like her meal.

As it was with this physical meal, the same is true in the spiritual meals of our lives. We rush through, glancing at the scriptures like grabbing little snacks, but never really sitting down to a satisfying word of God. We need a word meal that fills our spirit with warmth, wholeness, and complete comfort.

Just as we are hungry again within the hours of eating our last meal in our physical body, our spirits are just as hungry or more. God knew we would understand hunger for food. Have you ever found yourself just unsatisfied? Uncertain? Unfulfilled? God has a word that will fill you up and satisfy all your needs (not wants all the time, but definitely your needs). Just as with your physical hunger, you will grow hungry again spiritually.

They say we mistake our physical hunger sometimes for thirst. We mistake our spiritual hunger so many times for something our flesh is screaming out for like an emotional need or a need for a feeling, but in reality we are thirsty for a drink of something way more satisfying than a drink or a meal. We need a comforting word that will stick with us and a drink of his living word to quench our fleshly thirst.

Come with me to Matt 5:6 & John 4:13-14

Blessed fortunate, well off, happy **are those who hunger** to crave, starving **and thirst for righteousness** innocent, holy, just, meet with GOD, **for they will be filled** satisfied.

Jesus answered, "Everyone who drinks this water will be thirsty again, but whoever drinks the water I give him HIS WORD is LIVING WATER, it fills constantly, BUT you have to drink it, read it, listen to Him, obey Him and His Word, DO IT. If you take those actions look what He promises **will never thirst. Indeed, the water I give him will become in him a spring of water welling up to eternal life."**

What I learned:

Please hear me on this: This is simple; this relationship with God is as simple as talking to him, seeking him through reading his word, being around other believers (they will not be perfect Christians; this is a journey, not a sprint). When you are unsatisfied, hungry, and thirsty for something more than a piece of bread (or big piece of your favorite cake) or a drink of water (whole milk, not skim!), there is the Holy Spirit just waiting to come in and fill you with the warmth of peace, understanding, comfort, love, joy and goodness. You may be in the worst situation, but when you turn to the Holy Spirit to feed your emotional hunger, you will satisfy in your deepest hunger, your soul. Don't try to understand it; let him teach you by spending time with him, eating his word, and filling your cup by worshipping him.

Your turn in the Word:

"Never again will they _____; never again will they _____. The sun will _____ beat upon them, nor any scorching heat. For the Lamb at the center of the throne will be their shepherd; he will_____ them to springs of _____ water. And God will wipe away every _____ from their eyes" (Revelation 7:16-17).

_____

_____

_____

Thinking of Others ...

My Comforter, how precious it is, Lord, to know that you are thinking about my family, friends, and people I don't know, constantly! I can't even count the number of times a day your thoughts go out toward them. Let them come to your "kitchen" for food and water. Give them a desire to want to feast with you every moment of every day.

_____

_____

_____

Repentance ...

Jesus, I need forgiveness for running to the things of this world to quench my thirst and hunger. I get it so wrong, and I often know it when I am doing it. Please forgive my rebellious mind that leads to rebellious, un-Christ like actions. I choose to change; through one meal at a time (of your word), I will learn and grow.

_____

_____

_____

My Desires ...

My helper, please give me the desire to run to you for spiritual food rather than to others, things, food, and all the cheap replacements of this world that gives me temporary comfort. I long to have comfort and peace by being in relationship with you every second of the day.

_____

_____

_____

Write down a person, place, or thing that you could avoid going to for comfort today; instead go to God with your words and read his as well.

Day #15:
SPEAK HIS NAME

The Sense of Humor Spot:

A little boy was in a relative's wedding. As he was coming down the aisle he would take two steps, stop, and turn to the crowd (alternating between bride's side and groom's side), put his hands up like claws, and roar. Step, step, ROAR, step step, ROAR, all the way down the aisle.

The crowd was near tears from laughing so hard by the time he reached the pulpit. The little boy, however, was getting more and more distressed from all the laughing and was almost crying by the time he reached the pulpit. When asked what he was doing, the child sniffed and said, "I was being the Ring Bear."

WORD

I am so thankful for children. I hear the voice of God in their thoughts. Children are not tainted like we as adults can be. Their thoughts are usually pure and honest because they don't have all the memories, the hurts, the things of life to filter their thoughts through. They just say what they think.

I had a beautiful teaching moment with a child who taught me how simple it is to find immediate comfort in my situations. Sitting in my lap, she began this conversation about being scared and asking me what I do when I get scared. Knowing that she wasn't a walking s-Word (Bible) and that she didn't really know a lot of scriptures off the top of her head to speak to those fears (neither did I until I started writing this book), I told her that the way to stop those fearful thoughts was to just speak the name of Jesus.

She asked, "Well, what if I am at school and I am scared. What should I do or say?" I answered her by just simply naming who God was and asked her to give me names she thought described God. It went something like this as I began, "Father, Comforter, Healer, Spirit of Truth, Redeemer, Counselor" then she joined in and said, "Son, Jesus, Love."

As bright as a child's face could shine, as her shoulders went from tense to relaxed, she said, "Awwww, that feels better!"

She experienced that just speaking those names of truth comforted her in an instant.

She didn't have to know the books of the Bible or a scripture memorized to a T. She just needed the name of Jesus, and so did I.

COME WITH ME TO JEREMIAH 10:6, NLT

Lord, there is no one like you! No one is like God. In your times of fear, doubt, trouble, or even gladness, happiness, and true joy, call on God! **For You are great** He is much mightier. He is noble. He is the highest tower! He lifts you up! **and your name is full of power.** Just speaking his name gives us power!

WHAT I LEARNED:

When we call on Jesus and speak all the names of who he is and the names about his character, we begin to feel immediate release of a power greater than us working to relieve our worries or to share in our times of joy. You know there are times when others can't even rejoice with us, but the King of Kings is just waiting to have a party with us. Just start speaking his name.

YOUR TURN IN THE WORD:

"He who dwells in the shelter of the _____ High will rest in the shadow of the _____. I will say of the LORD, 'He is my _____ and my _____, in whom I trust'" (Psalm 91:1-2).

_____

_____

_____

Thinking of Others ...

Most High God, you are our refuge and fortress. Nothing is too big for you. Please reveal who you are to us so that we will have praises of who you are on the tip of our tongues.

_____

_____

Repentance ...

O God, I know I grieve you when I call on other things and people to help me "get through" the day. All I have to do is call on your name, yet instead I rely on position, people, places, and things, thinking they will get me through. All I need is a real relationship with you. I am choosing to totally rely on you!

My Desires ...

You are my Strong Tower, my Refuge, my Counselor, my Prince of Peace, my Lord, my Master, my Comfort, my Foundation, my Deliverer, my Healer. You are my Everything. God, I want to know that I know you in such a way that I call only on your name. No one else, nothing else; just you!

Write down names that describe who God is to you. Has he healed you? Has he helped you? Has he given you anything?

Day #16:
UNDERSTAND WITH
YOUR HEART

The Sense of Humor Spot:
Q. If you're American in the kitchen, what are you in the bathroom?
A. European.

WORD

Have you ever understood something with your heart, but not with your head or mind? Maybe you understood something with your intellect, but not in your heart? If we are ever going to truly know God, we have to get understanding of his word in our hearts, not just our heads or intellectual minds.

Take, for instance, the word love. One description of the word love is affectionate concern for the well-being of others. I understand that definition in my mind and my intellect, but if my heart cannot show affectionate concern for others well-being, then that word is only partially understood by me. My heart has to understand just like my head does.

It's like a really cute kid, I mean, adorable. Then that really sweet-looking, adorable kid bites you, stomps on your toes, and says some naughty words. It just doesn't line up. He's looks a certain way, but acts another.

That is what it looks like when we don't gain understanding of the word. It looks and sounds good, but if we do not show understanding of the word by acting upon what we see, hear, and learn with our hearts, then we don't really know what it means.

Come with me to Acts 28:25-27

They disagreed among themselves and began to leave after Paul had made this final statement: "The Holy Spirit spoke the truth to your forefathers when he said through Isaiah the prophet: 'Go to this people and say, "You will be ever hearing, but never understanding; How many times have you heard a scripture, but you never really understood it? you will be ever seeing but never perceiving." Have you ever seen a word, knew what it sounded like and looked like, but were not sure what it meant? I always keep a dictionary with me. My kids are starting to say words that I never heard before. I would rather look stupid trying to understand than to not understand at all. For this people's heart has become calloused; Most of the time it is easier to just move on over a word we read or that is spoken to us. We become insensitive to it and what it is trying to tell us. they hardly hear with their ears, We hear, but not enough to turn and truly listen. and they have closed their eyes. You know that expression, "Just close your eyes and when you open them, it will be gone"? That is what we think sometimes.

'Otherwise Other = different. Wise = having the power of discerning and judging properly as to what is true or right. they might see with their eyes, Wanting to see the truth is powerful. hear with their ears, Hearing the truth sets you on a path to freedom. understand to be thoroughly familiar with (God's character) with their hearts, Heart = the innermost or central part of anything. The center of emotion. The center of intellect. and turn, If you are going south on the interstate (of life) and you want to go north, you have to turn around, make a u-turn, go the other direction. and I would heal Heal = free from evil; cleanse; purify. To become whole or sound. them.' Them — that's you and me. He will set us free from evil, cleanse us, make us whole and sound if we see with our eyes, listen to his truth with our ears, and get understanding with our hearts. Also, we have to make a turn. Some of us may take a u-turn and live our lives with the Holy Spirit directing us. Then there are those of us who take the w-route. We go the wrong direction, let's say south for a little while, then we turn back north by lining our right choices up with the word. Then we turn again and go back south by returning to our bad choices and so forth. Hopefully, we will all end up going north and bring our friends and families with us.

What I learned:

I can't just understand the Father, the Son, and the Holy Spirit with my head knowledge and intellect. I also have to understand with my heart. God's ways are ways that you can't wrap your intellectual mind around because God is so awesome, he doesn't want to just be confined to knowledge. He wants relationship. We all know that when we are in relationship, there are things that happen that you can't wrap your intellect around! When I understand with my heart what love truly is, then I know how to give it. How can I truly give something if I can't understand it?

Your turn in the Word:

"For the _____ gives _____, and from his mouth comes knowledge and understanding" (Proverbs 2:6).

_____

_____

_____

Thinking of Others ...

Wisdom, rain down on my friends and family. Let truth be understood in our hearts and not just in our heads. Give us the desire to slow down enough to really get understanding of your words. God, give us eyes to see your truth. Give us ears to hear your truth. Give us hearts that want to understand and not fight you, but understand you.

_____

_____

_____

Repentance ...

Father of Truth, I run from your understanding because I want to do things my way, on my timetable, and with my effort. The truth is that when I get your understanding life becomes so much simpler. The more time I spend with you day by day, moment by moment, the more you free me from the things that bring me temporary fulfillment, and yet long-term guilt and suffering. Understanding your truth sets me free! God, give me grace. I will change.

_____

_____

My Desires ...

My true Friend, I really want to *under-* (below, beneath) *stand* (bear, endure, position, halt, to remain firm or steadfast, to assume or keep an upright position on the feet) you. When I remain under your authority, you make me stand firmly in an upright position. I long to understand you.

Understanding is a process. It takes time. Remember going to school? They didn't give you an algebra book in kindergarten. No, you have to understand little by little. Don't get discouraged.

What is something that you really never had a true understanding of? Who could you ask to help you understand?

God will help you understand his words. Just keep seeking!

Day #17:
WHEN LIES BECOME
THE TRUTH

The Sense of Humor Spot:

A clergyman was walking down the street when he came upon a group of about a dozen boys, all of them between 10 and 12 years of age. The group was circled around a dog. Concerned the boys were hurting the dog, the clergyman went over and asked, "What are you doing with that dog?" One of the boys replied, "This dog is just an old neighborhood stray. We all want him, but only one of us can take him home. So we've decided that whichever one of us can tell the biggest lie will get to keep the dog."

The reverend was taken aback. "You boys shouldn't be having a contest telling lies!" he exclaimed. He then launched into a 10-minute sermon against lying, beginning, "Don't you boys know it's a sin to lie?" and ending with, "Why, when I was your age, I never told a lie."

There was dead silence for about a minute. Just as the reverend was beginning to think he'd gotten through to them, the smallest boy gave a deep sigh and said, "All right, give him the dog."

WORD

The Webster's unabridged dictionary describes a lie as a false statement made with deliberate intent to deceive; an intentional untruth; something intended or serving to convey a false impression; to imply falsity of. To speak falsely or utter untruth knowingly, as with intent to deceive.

Everybody lies at some point in their lives. We start lying around age 4 or 5 to test boundaries and see if telling a lie can get us out of trouble. It is not malicious; it just goes back to Adam and Eve. Truly, that is where our sin nature started. The problem is when one lie becomes another lie and pretty soon the little white lies have turned you into a person no one can trust, and deep down, you can't even trust yourself.

See if you can recognize any of these lies you might be telling yourself unknowingly or perhaps someone else might be saying to you:

"I am not enough, not smart enough, not skinny enough, not Christian enough."

"You're not doing enough. You don't have true friends. You don't belong anywhere. You are better off alone."

"I am not rich enough; or I don't deserve all that I have."

"You are not being a good wife. What kind of mom are you? You'll never make it. What makes you think you can make it in that school or group?"

Or, the pride lies, I think we don't really think we say them, but perhaps we may do so unknowingly:

"I am just too good for that. I have it all together. I am just so much better off by myself. I would never do that!"

Or what about the little lies we might tell others about someone else or a particular situation.

"I know deep down that if I say this one tiny, no big deal 'story' about a person or situation, it will make me look better, but it's not the whole truth."

I've been there, and I have told myself some of those lies. Pitiful, I know. How about you? As I have begun to understand truth, I am very cautious about things I say or do to others. I do what I want them to do to me.

So, if I want to be lied about, all I have to do is lie about someone else or something else. I get the fruit from the type of tree I plant. If I want to bear an apple tree, I plant apple seeds. If I plant a word of doubt, I will reap doubt.

My list of lies goes on, on, and on. Whether good or bad, you can get so full on your own lies. (Unfortunately, in my life those lies started to become my truth.) It wasn't until I starting seeking out God's truth in his

73

scripture, in talking with him everyday, in walking in truth with friends who were also seeking out truth that I began to see the lies that I had believed, spoken, heard for so long about myself and others. I especially watch out for my thoughts about myself. Are my thoughts are not lining up with the scripture in Philippians 4:8 — "Finally, my sisters and my brothers, whatever is true, whatever is noble, whatever is right, whatever is pure, whatever is lovely, whatever is admirable-if anything is excellent or praiseworthy — think about such things"?

P.S.: We are flesh and blood. We are humans who are going to make mistakes. We may say something that is a false statement about ourselves or someone else because we are fleshly. We have to always be living in the spirit and in truth in order not to let one another down. Relationships are so hard at times and so good at times, but one thing is for sure relationships are. They are necessary, essential, and needed.

Come with me to Psalm 119:28-30

My soul is weary with sorrow; We will face times of sorrow; that is a fact. **strengthen me according to your word.** Just one word of encouragement can change your outlook. **Keep me from deceitful ways;** This is written because we have been lying to ourselves since Adam and Eve. Denial about truth is deadly. **be gracious to me through your law.** It is a privilege to have instruction such as the law. Imagine a child who never had instruction or a computer that never had a program. Instructions are vital. Don't run from them. Read them; then do them.

I always want to skip over the manual. Seriously, it's a problem. When I take the time to slow down enough to find out how something works, I actually know what to do. We can't know how this life works if we don't read our manual, the Bible. It teaches you what buttons to push and how to operate. When we know how to operate something, it brings us joy. It's when we don't know how to work something that we become frustrated and want to give up and throw up our hands in defeat. My Bible says I am his glory, so I am thinking his glory would be a V-I-C-T-O-R-Y story. You know I want to cheer that! **I have chosen the way of truth;** The way of truth is a choice. God will not force us to be faithful. You choose faithfulness because of your relationship with him. **I have set my heart on your laws.** You have to understand that regulations keep you regular.

What I Learned:

In this life, we have two choices: life or death. Every time I choose to lie, even just a tiny bit, I have chosen death. You see, those little bitty lies start multiplying, and they start becoming truth.

When lies become truth, the world around us is so confusing. We don't trust anyone; we are anxious and shaky. Who can have real relationships without truth? I choose life by learning, living, and following the instructions of God. What we feed grows. If I feed myself truth by being in some BS (Bible study) in the word of God, my heart gets tender, my actions change, and I don't feel like I have to lie to please others. Truth begins to sink in my heart, and then I can begin to spot a lie from a mile away.

When you spot a lie, you have a word of truth to speak over that lie. Just think — if we all walked around telling the truth, no more guessing, no more backstabbing, no more hurting. Truth sets us free!

Your turn in the Word:

"The Lord _____ lying lips, but he delights in those who tell the _____" (Proverbs 12:22).

_____

_____

_____

Thinking of Others ...

Do not let us be deceived, Lord. Let us see, understand, and know truth so that we may live in truth. Give us a hunger for your instruction and a desire to live inside your regulations.

_____

_____

_____

Repentance ...

My Redeemer, the worst lies I have told have been the ones I have told myself about myself. Please forgive me for not understanding or knowing who I am in you. Only you, Father, and my true friends can give me truth.

_____

_____

My Desires ...

Father of truth, it is my desire to walk so closely in your truth that I can identify a lie as soon as it is spoken and take that thought captive and speak words of truth immediately so those lies cannot go beyond my mind to my heart, or a lie cannot come to me from someone else and even get in my mind. Let me be so aware of your truth that it is so simple, so right, and so immediate.

_____

_____

_____

Think of just one lie you have told yourself. Now, right now, speak truth over it. For instance, we say "I just can't overcome this."

Luke 18:27 (NLT), says, "He [Jesus] replied, "What is impossible for people is possible with God."

Day #18:
OLD DIRTY DEVIL

The Sense of Humor Spot:

There was a Christian lady who lived next door to an atheist. Every day, when the lady prayed, the atheist guy could hear her. He thought to himself, "She sure is crazy, praying all the time like that. Doesn't she know there isn't a God?"

Many times while she was praying, he would go to her house and harass her, saying "Lady, why do you pray all the time? Don't you know there is no God?" But she kept on praying.

One day, she ran out of groceries. As usual, she was praying to the Lord explaining her situation and thanking Him for what he was going do. As usual, the atheist heard her praying and thought to himself, "Humph! I'll fix her."

He went to the grocery store, bought a whole bunch of groceries, took them to her house, dropped them off on the front porch, rang the door bell, and then hid in the bushes to see what she would do. When she opened the door and saw the groceries, she began to praise the Lord with all her heart, jumping, singing and shouting everywhere! The atheist then jumped out of the bushes and told her, "You ol' crazy lady, God didn't buy you those groceries; I bought those groceries!"

At hearing this, she broke out and started running down the street, shouting and praising the Lord. When he finally caught her, he asked what her problem was.

She said, "I knew the Lord would provide me with some groceries, but I didn't know he was gonna make the devil pay for them!"

WORD

The first thing that old dirty devil is after is my mind. He is always looking for ways to get me to do something I think I want to do, but deep down I know is not right. It is tough to spot sometimes, but that is why the Bible describes that old dirty devil as cunning and tricky. Look at the story of Eve in the Garden. The first thing the serpent said to the woman, "Did God really say, 'You must not eat from any tree in the garden?'" He didn't throw a great big arrow in between her eyeballs. He took the truth and slowly got her to doubt truth, to get her to do what he wanted her to do.

And so she got temporary satisfaction, but that little twist of truth began the fall of man. I know good from evil. I know when I am doing good or evil. I know deep down in my spirit when God tells me to do or not to do something, but I begin to conveniently make excuses that will "fit" my temporary indulgence. Oh, how many times I have and still do fall into this trap of excuses.

Thankfully, because of understanding truth, these lapses are getting further apart. Those excuses will eventually catch up with me and when God comes looking for me, I hide in denial. Thank God he sent his Son, Jesus, to set us free from our excuses and denial. The key to freedom is real sorrow for past sin, asking God to forgive us, and turning the right direction (The right direction is sometimes the direction you want to avoid the most!) It is so simple, so freeing; yet so many of us hang onto our past sin, never ask for forgiveness, and continue in that overwhelming state of guilt.

Come with me to Genesis 3:1-7

Now the serpent was more crafty (cunning, deceitful) than any of the wild animals the LORD God had made. He said to the woman, "Did God really say, 'You must not eat from any tree in the garden'?" This question should be a red flag for you. When you begin to question something about what God is telling you to do or not to do, that is when you have to get silent and ask God to show you his truth for that situation, pray, and seek out scriptures for answers. If you don't have a clear answer from God, don't act on that situation until you do or only act on what you know is right.

The woman said to the serpent, "We may eat fruit from the trees in the garden, but God did say, 'You must not eat fruit from the tree that is in the middle of the garden, and you must not touch it, or you will die.'" She already knew God's boundaries in the garden. We have boundaries called the Ten Commandments and the two that Jesus gave when he came to earth, which are, first, "Love the Lord your God with all your heart and with all your soul and with all your mind," and second, "Love your neighbor as yourself." When making a choice, ask yourself, "Is this within God's boundaries?"

"You will not surely die," the serpent said to the woman. "For God knows that when you eat of it, your eyes will be opened, and you will be like God, knowing good and evil." There that old dirty devil goes, putting an idea in her mind that she would know more than God. We listen to that lie daily when we do what we want rather than listening to God, his truth, his boundaries, his principles, and his promises. I've got some work to do on learning all his principles and promises that I know will bring me freedom, true happiness, and complete peace.

When the woman saw that the fruit of the tree was good for food and pleasing to the eye, and also desirable for gaining wisdom, Some questions to ask yourself if you are tempted to do something God specifically told you in your heart not to do: "Is this pleasing to the eye? Am I doing this to gain wisdom outside of God? Am I taking on too much to please the people around me? Am I at peace with my choices?" Usually, your first instinct is correct, but is soon overridden with excuses to fit our wants and fleshly desires. she took some and ate it. She also gave some to her husband, We will find people who will do what we know we shouldn't, because it feels better when we reason, "If they do it, then so can I." who was with her, and he ate it. Then the eyes of both of them were opened, and they realized they were naked; so they sewed fig leaves together and made coverings for themselves. How many times have I really seen the naked truth of my crazy choices and tried to cover them up or sweep them under the rug so I don't have to see those choices for what they really are?

What I Learned:

That old dirty devil is after our mind, our rational thinking. He begins to ever so slightly give you excuses and lies that will help you make choices to go against what is right and good for you. The more you choose to listen to his deceptive voice of excuses and lies, the more bad choices you make. As a result, we have more guilt, more shame, and the more we find "fig leaves." Money, jobs that take all our time from our families, sex, possessions, people, trying to look perfect on the outside, drugs/alcohol, selfishness, laziness, out-of-control shopping, gossiping, and so much more to cover ourselves up.

The answer is truly asking God moment by moment, day by day for forgiveness. Listen, it is when you identify your problem that you can find a solution. The first step is going to God for help. He will help you if your heart is asking, seeking, and knocking on his door, but you have to want to have solutions. No one can do this thing called "life" for you. It's up to you!

Your turn in the Word:

"But encourage one another daily, as long as it is called _____, so that none of you may be hardened by _____ deceitfulness" (Hebrews 3:13).

_____

_____

_____

Thinking of Others ...

Father, I know this is one of the toughest areas in our lives — believing that old dirty devil's cunning lies and doing what we know we shouldn't do. Please give special grace to all of us who need you and your truth in our particular situations. Don't let them hear the lies of that old dirty devil, but only let them hear truth and do it.

_____

_____

_____

Repentance ...

Lord, I give thanks in my repentance because I know it's when I come to you and tell you what I've done, totally, that I can begin to be set free. So I thank you for revealing to me that I have believed lies and have acted on them. I try to cover up my sin with other things. Lord, I humbly come before you and ask your truth to be known in my heart. I turn to you, not to the lies of that old dirty devil.

_____

_____

_____

My Desires .....

God, you are good. I want to replace lies with what is good and true. The minute I give myself an excuse to do something that I know I shouldn't, help me make the right choice in that moment and enjoy the freedom, happiness, love, joy, and so many other blessings that come from just listening to your voice. Let me not make life so complicated by making excuses for things that look good to my flesh and make me think there is wisdom beyond you that I can gain.

_____

_____

_____

Can you think of a time when you knew the right thing, but you talked yourself into doing the wrong thing? Don't forget to write or draw how you covered it up.

Facing your past sin could get ugly, but think about the cocoon of a butterfly. It's pretty ugly in the process of change, but what comes out of that cocoon is rare, beautiful, colorful, and flies! When you let go of that ugly cocoon of lies, hurt, and self-deceit in order to trust, listen, seek, and understand who you truly are (rare, beautiful, and colorful), you begin to fly with freedom!

Day #19:
INTIMACY

The Sense of Humor Spot:

A big-game hunter went on safari with his wife and mother-in-law. One evening, while still deep in the jungle, the wife awoke to find her mother gone. Rushing to her husband, she insisted on them both trying to find her mother.

The hunter picked up his rifle, took a swig of whiskey, and started to look for her. In a clearing not far from the camp, they came upon a chilling sight. The mother-in-law was backed up against a thick, impenetrable bush, and a large male lion stood facing her.

The wife cried, "What are we going to do?"

"Nothing," said the hunter husband. "The lion got himself into this mess; let him get himself out of it."

WORD

Intimacy — a quality or expression of familiarity, affection, love, or passion associated in close personal relations. This word is one of the best words on earth! Why? It gives a complete understanding of what a relationship with God looks and feels like. Intimacy with God is so beautiful because like the word begins, intimacy goes and comes from the inner personal relationship. It is not based on the outer person; otherwise it would be called "outerimacy" (my new word). Intimacy goes into your heart and searches out affections, love, and passion. Intimacy is often thought of as having a sexual relationship.

Some of us think of the word intimacy and think, "Yuck, I would rather clean dog vomit than get intimate." You know what I mean. That wasn't a question, because I know you know. This intimacy with the King of Kings is so deep, so real, so mysterious, so engaging, so detailed, and so a place of deep understanding. Not only are you understood, but you begin to understand him.

The picture I want to paint for you is a wedding ceremony where this bride-to-be and groom are so in love. The beautiful bride is standing before her husband-to-be. The only thing that separates them is her veil. The vows have been made and the "I do's" flew; then came time for the intimacy, the kiss. As the groom goes to kiss his bride, she won't raise her veil and let him come into a close, real, deep relationship with him. She says the vows, but stops the groom at the veil. She keeps him separated by not raising the veil and letting her groom in.

That is a picture of our relationship with Christ. We say we accept our vows with him. We want him in our lives. We want a relationship with him. We say "I do." Then we stop right there. We hardly communicate with Him. We barely spend time with Him. Or, we get so caught up with the laws of religion that we forget to have that intimate relationship filled with grace and mercy that Jesus came to offer.

You can't have a relationship with someone if you feel like they are constantly judging you or condemning you. Or, maybe you can, but I am not sure I see the intimacy being based on love in that situation. Remove the veil we put between us and a true intimate relationship with God. Get some lovin' in your oven, for goodness sake. I know I am!

Come with me to II Corinthians 3:15-17

Even to this day when Moses is read, a veil covers their hearts. This is just my opinion, but I believe "the veil that covers their hearts" is the law. Jesus came to fulfill the law. Now because of Jesus, the law is covered with mercy and grace. We have the Ten Commandments to guide us into truth. We also have the two commandments that Jesus gave ... to love the Lord God with all your heart and to love one another as yourself.

I don't know about you, but if I expect my family and friends to follow the law to the letter, I am fooling myself. The only way to even get close to following the Ten Commandments is through grace and mercy, and that only comes through having a relationship with Christ.

Jesus said, "Love one another as yourself." If I am walking around judging others where they fall short of the Ten Commandments, I, too, have failed in having an intimate relationship with Christ. It is not for me to judge, but love, just as I would want to be loved. Jesus said that, I didn't.

But whenever anyone turns to the Lord, It says turns to the Lord, not Law. **the veil is taken away.** Let the party of true intimacy begin. **Now the Lord is the Spirit, and where the Spirit of the Lord is, there is**

freedom. There is freedom, because he writes the laws on your heart moment by moment. When you are walking with the spirit of God through an intimate relationship with him, the veil of anything we put between God and ourselves is removed through a relationship with the Holy Spirit.

What I learned:

Intimacy with God comes through lifting the veil we put in between ourselves and God. I choose to lift my veil of all my preconceptions of following this law or that method, and I run to the intimate arms of the Holy Spirit.

Your turn in the Word:

"But their _____ were made dull, for to this day the same veil remains when the _____ covenant is read. It has _____ been removed, because only _____ Christ is it taken away" (II Corinthians 3:14).

_____

_____

_____

Thinking of Others...

Lavish Lover of intimacy, we come to you and ask you to lift our veils. Let us see with mercy and grace, the way you intended it to be when you sent your Son to fulfill the law. Let us know the intimacy that comes out of a relationship of sharing time walking, talking, singing, loving, listening, crying, laughing, seeing, and so much more, through the lifted veil of the Holy Spirit. Break the chains of religion and give us freedom in your innermost places of intimacy.

_____

_____

_____

Repentance ...

Creator of me, you have watched me try to figure out how to have a relationship with you. I have failed miserably at times because I wouldn't lift my veil of self-righteousness from between us. I let myself believe I could follow your laws on my own. I know it is only through an intimate relationship with you that your love and mercy can even get me close to knowing who you really are. Forgive me for judging others instead of looking at the telephone pole sticking out of my own eyeball.

_____

_____

_____

My Desires ...

    My Man, my Man, I want some intimacy with you. I want to feel you breathe on me. I want to listen to your voice whisper sweet nothings in my ear. I want to tell you some juicy stuff, too. I want to laugh, cry, love, sing, dance, and live this life with each other. "I do!"

_____

_____

_____

    Do you have a veil between you and God? Draw a picture of you, a veil, and a visual of God. What does your veil look like? Is it doubt, fear, an issue of trust, rebellion, or religion, saying you can't love like that, or uncertainty of the unknown?

Day #20:
YOU SPEAK CHRISTIAN?

The Sense of Humor Spot:

A mother mouse and a baby mouse are walking along, when all of a sudden, a cat attacks them. The mother mouse goes, "BARK!" and the cat runs away.

"See?" says the mother mouse to her baby. "Now do you see why it's important to learn a foreign language?"

WORD

Have you ever been to a foreign country only to realize you are the only one in that country who could not understand a thing that was going on? Or have you tried to communicate with someone who speaks a foreign language? It's funny how people try to communicate in these situations by yelling. Uhhh… the problem is not their hearing! Even sign language — you see mouths or hands moving, and you know you should understand, and you want to understand so much, but it's just not coming to you.

Well, I have, and it is confusing and way out of my comfort zone. It's frustrating work trying to understand a language you don't understand. You might know a word here or there from the different language and continually repeat it (which is worse), but the rest is as clear as mud. Well, my friend, that is what being a Christian is like, especially in this world today. I so get it now. See, I was raised by seeing, learning, and understanding what a lifestyle of Christianity is meant to be.

I understand how difficult it must look for so many. There are so many ways to speak that language. Some Christians are so faithful to the language. They speak it and act it out fully. Then there are those who get a little lazy in their language and take shortcuts and chop up the Christian language.

86

But remember, speaking a new language is a lifestyle and a journey of learning. A process of failing, but then growth. This is true with many languages. In my experience with the Spanish language, I think you can say one word five different ways. Eeekkk; so confusing. I end up feeling like an idiot for even trying. Then I realize that I would at least want someone to try to understand me if I were trying to tell them something. You see, God is trying to talk to you in your language. He wants to understand you and for you to understand him. The only way for us to understand something or someone is to study it or them.

How do you learn? You read, you listen, and you go places that will help expand your knowledge so that you will have understanding. You try and you work at building relationships that will help you speak the Christian language.

I tried to learn Spanish before I went to Peru, and I learned a few words, but when I went to Peru and hung around the Peruvians and their language, I understood and knew more words than I ever would just trying to learn on my own. It's the same with the Christian language; you have to find Christians who are speaking the language in their lives that you want for your life, like love, joy, peace, patience, kindness, goodness, faithfulness, gentleness, and self control.

Come with me to I Corinthians 14:9-11

So it is with you. **Unless you speak intelligible words with your tongue, how will anyone know what you are saying? You will just be speaking into the air. Undoubtedly there are all sorts of languages in the world,** How many languages do you speak? **yet none of them is without meaning.** Do you understand the language or languages that you speak? **If then I do not grasp the meaning of what someone is saying, I am a foreigner to the speaker, and he is a foreigner to me.** I don't know about you, but I do not want to be a foreigner to the God who created me. I want to learn his language through studying his word, his character, his sense of humor. I just want to understand him because I know he understands me, and he created me.

What I learned:

Learning to speak the Christian language is foreign at first, like anything you first attempt. It is uncomfortable to be around other people who are speaking to one another in a language I don't understand. Being in a church and seeing people raise their hands in worship or doing a Bible Study and not having a clue that there is even a book in the Bible called Nahum.

I've been there, believe me. Don't be overwhelmed. This is a process. I have to remind myself of this. I mean, for goodness sake, I am writing this book, and I have a ton of stuff I that I am still working on and have so much to learn. But, what I do know is that I have a personal relationship with God. And that, my friend, is all you need to get started in speaking and living this Christian language. It is in the doing of this language that you begin to truly understand how beautiful it is to be able to speak Christian. Don't get caught up on one "word"; just keep learning and seeking his language, which, by the way, is always a love language.

YOUR TURN IN THE WORD:

"If I speak in the tongues of men and of angels, but have not _____, I am only a resounding gong or a clanging cymbal. If I have the gift of prophecy and can fathom all mysteries and all knowledge, and if I have a faith that can move mountains, but have not _____, I am _____. If I give all I possess to the poor and surrender my body to the flames, but have not _____, I gain _____" (1 Corinthians 13:1-3).

_____

_____

_____

Thinking of Others ...

Most High, we know that everyone on this earth can learn the "Christian language." God, give us a desire to learn about you, your language, your culture, your lifestyle, and how to carry on a relationship with you. You speak everyone's language. You understand their hearts. You want to bring understanding to us. Give us a heart to want to learn to communicate with you. You speak the language of LOVE to everyone, no matter what nationality, age, or place they may be. You speak to us in our HEARTS.

_____

_____

_____

Repentance ...

Oh, Lord, the languages I have spoken. Who can count? I know you have forgiven me each time I have asked, and I will continue to ask you to forgive me when I speak a language or act in a way that is not what you intended the Christian lifestyle or language to look like or sound like.

_____

_____

_____

My Desires...

Language of Love, my God, I know your truest language is not just spoken, but the greatest language communicated is LOVE. Please teach me, use me, and guide me in speaking and giving the ultimate language, which is YOUR LOVE.

_____

_____

_____

Have you ever seen someone walk in this amazing grace and love? Do you speak Christian?

Day #21:
WHAT PLEASES MY MAN

The Sense of Humor Spot:
Bob was in trouble. He forgot his wedding anniversary. His wife was really steamed! She told him, "Tomorrow morning, I expect to find a gift in the driveway that goes from 0 to 200 in 6 seconds, and it better be there!!"

The next morning he got up early and left for work. When his wife woke up, she looked out the window, and sure enough, there was a gift-wrapped box in the middle of the driveway. Confused, the wife put on her robe, ran out to the driveway, and brought the box back in the house.

She opened it and found a brand new bathroom scale. Bob has been missing since Friday.

WORD

Have you felt scared to do something, but knew that if you took a step forward you would be OK? You might fall, you might skin your knees, or you might get embarrassed. You knew anything could happen, but you were willing to go forward.

Faith, along with obeDIEnce, taking action, and loving are what please God the most. Faith is being sure of what we hope for and certain of what we cannot see.

When is the last time you sat down in a chair? Did you look it over and check its sturdiness, or did you just plop down having faith that it would hold you? Please don't complicate, question, or get all theological about faith.

Simplicity is the key to faith. Just come as a child and believe in God, his promises, his words and his guidance. Faith comes by hearing the good news of the simple message of Jesus Christ. I have never doubted the simple message, and I thank God for that gift.

I do know that the more I ask, seek, and knock on the door of the word of God by being in a family of believers that consists of many different people and places, by reading the word every day, having a heart of worship, singing, by taking some actions that totally took faith to take, my faith is becoming like the mustard seed that Jesus used as a model for the kingdom of God. Initially, the mustard seed starts off by being the smallest seed, but grows to be the biggest of all garden plants.

Nothing, especially faith, can grow if you don't water it. You have to be as purposeful to water and feed your faith as you do your face! Just as you hunger for food every three to four hours, we need to feed our spirits food. We are starving our faith. We need some faith food all day, every day!

Like when you eat junk food, the more junk you eat, the more your face breaks out, your bootie gets big, and you feel bad, but when you start eating fruit, vegetables, whole grains, and all those God-given foods, your skin begins to radiate.

It's the same in your spirit. When you feed your spirit junk, you begin to doubt, you question faith, and you feel bad. When you feed yourself faith food from the Scriptures, your skin begins to radiate, you begin to look young and full of life, your actions are more intentional, and your steps of faith become more consistent. Pretty soon your mustard seed (your dreams, your hopes) becomes so big, you forget it all just started with a seed — one small step of faith.

What covers all that is love. Love covers a multitude of sins; love is the blanket of hope. Giving love pleases my Man.

Come with me to Hebrews 11:1-3

Now faith is being sure of what we hope for What are you hoping for? What are your expectations? Why are you limiting GOD? **and certain of what we do not see. This is what the ancients were commended for.**

By faith we understand that the universe was formed at God's command, a word created the universe. What word has God given you today? We are made in his likeness. We were meant to create. Build your faith today by creating something you can't see because of what you hope for, whether that's a home, a relationship, a garden, an environment of love, or something else that reflects his glory **so that what is seen was not made out of what was visible.**

What I learned:

What pleases God is faith, faith in his Son, Jesus Christ, who came to this earth and lived among people like you and me. He died on a cross for my sins and yours so that we would have eternal life. Faith is my everything. I have stepped out in faith on things like leaving old ways of living to new ways, reaching out to find new friends, and marrying a man I didn't really know (to now realize that he is my best friend). I have delivered two children, built two homes, overcome breast cancer twice, and written this book. Faith. Step after faith-step.

See, you have to be willing to fail, fall, get dirty, have people laugh at you, and take criticism to enjoy the victories, the fulfillment of dreams, the rich relationships. To enjoy this life to the fullest, you have to have faith.

Your turn in the Word:

"Consequently, faith comes from _____ the message, and the message is _____ through the word of Christ" (Romans 10:17).

_____

_____

_____

Thinking of Others …

Father of faith, give us faith to trust you even when we don't see the "big picture." Give us moments of faith-food, faith that will make us grow and learn to trust you completely. You are who your word says you are!

_____

_____

_____

Repentance …

Jesus, there have been times when I have said, "I have faith!" — only to say in the same sentence, "Give me faith to believe." God, you are sovereign, you never change. I am sorry for making excuses instead of taking steps that lead me to completely trust in YOU. Help me to do what you have told me to do. Faith is action in full motion!

_____

_____

_____

My Desires …

Light a fire in my soul so that when the aroma reaches you; it looks, smells, and acts like faith. I want to trust you so much that when an obstacle comes, I will rush to overcome through a word from you, a desire to fulfill the faith step you have called me to, and give you all the glory when I reach the other side.

_____

_____

_____

What step of faith have you been "trying to decide" to take? Leap, my friend, straight into his will for your life by taking the first step. It's like checkers: God is just waiting on you to make the first move; and right behind you, he moves and is waiting on your next move!

93

Day #22:
I JUST WANNA THANK YA!

The Sense of Humor Spot:

Several men are in the locker room of a golf club.

When a cell phone on a bench rings, a man engages the hands-free speaker function and begins to talk.

MAN: "Hello."

WOMAN: "Honey, it's me. Are you at the club?"

MAN: "Yes."

WOMAN: I am at the mall and found a beautiful leather coat. It's $1,000. Can I buy it?"

MAN: "OK, go ahead if you like it that much."

WOMAN: I also stopped by the Mercedes dealership and saw the latest models. I saw one I really liked. "

MAN: How much?"

WOMAN: $60,000.

MAN: "For that price, I want it with all the options."

WOMAN: "Great! One more thing: The house we wanted last year is back on the market. They're asking only $450,000."

MAN: "Well, then go ahead and buy it, but just offer $420,000."

WOMAN: "OK. I'll see you later! I love you!"

MAN: "Bye! I love you, too."

The man hangs up. The other men are looking at him in astonishment. Then he asks: "Anyone know who this phone belongs to?"

WORD

I can only tell you I have this thankfulness that is beyond natural understanding. This "thank you" is so deep, so pure, and so real. It comes from an understanding of where I have been and where I am now. It is a thankfulness that comes from knowing there is a plan and a purpose for me here. I have buried two friends (my own age) who suffered from the same disease I had. My thankfulness comes from knowing the relationship I have with the Lord is rare, yet available to everyone seeking. I am thankful for my family that is my everything, an ever-growing branch of friendships, a home that I could only have dreamed of living in, a desire to keep dreaming, a coffee pot to fill, a schedule to keep, and a life that will bring meaning. I have a heart of thankfulness.

Don't get me wrong, my thankful state of mind can be rearranged in a moment if you put me in a different location, but something I have always known and that will never change, no matter where I am, is the presence of the Lord.

It's God's grace in my life, I guess. He took me from a family of five living in a trailer house with no heat, no air conditioning, divorced parents, paying for Christian school tuition by wiping toilets and carrying

95

out a custodian's duties, to cleaning beautiful houses (little did I know that I would have an incredible house like those one day).

I couldn't comprehend a marriage to a man who had a degree from Texas Tech and a Super Bowl ring. For a little country girl like me, learning to be a student of women through doing nails and hair for many years, to having children (by the way, they didn't come with exact instructions with the stuff they sent home from the hospital), losing all my womanhood through a double mastectomy and chemotherapy, to losing my grandfather were a part of the journey God had planned for me. We even lost our dog, Kleats — our dog of 12 years, who taught me about being a mom before the real babies came. He delighted in the joys of bringing our two girls home; he saw me through those times of difficulty and taught me about the gift of "true" relationship.

That wasn't meant to be a pity story; that is my "God story" and the why for my heart of thankfulness that stems from all of those twists and turns in my life. You see, I have a thankful heart because I understand that what God is doing now is preparing me for what I need for tomorrow. It's easy to look down from the mountaintop and see where, when, and why, but it is hard to look up from the valley and be thankful for the mountaintop you haven't even seen.

If you want to be in the presence of God, you enter it through thanksgiving!

Come with me to Colossians 3:15

Let the peace of Christ rule in your hearts, What is ruling your heart? Are you more worried about what this person or that person thinks rather than what God thinks? You will never have peace in your heart if you are more concerned about fulfilling what others expect out of you than being concerned about what God expects out of you. **since as members of one body you were called** Called here means we are commanded or bid. **to peace.** We are called to quietness, rest, to be whole again. **And be thankful.** well-favored, grateful, thankful.

What I learned:

Please, if you hear one thing from this whole book, hear this: Thank him. Thank him for the trial: thank him for justice. Thank him for the valley. Thank him for the mountaintop. Thank him for where you are and where you are going, because without him breathing life into you, you would not even be here. I know your situation is so sad, so disgusting, so not like any other; but it is in those situations that he uses you and your situation for his glory to shine down in the valley so you can help someone else up to the mountaintop — only to look down in the valley to see how far you both came with God.

The quickest way out of a valley of negative thinking, anger, insecurity, hopelessness, loneliness, depression, or captivity of any kind is to reach out to someone else in the valley and pull them up. Somehow you end up coming up out of your valley, too. Something supernatural happens when you take the focus off of yourself and focus on someone else. If you don't believe me, try it!

Your turn in the Word

"The words 'once more' indicate the removing of what can be shaken — that is, created things — so that what _____ be shaken may remain. Therefore, since we are _____ a kingdom that cannot be _____, let us be thankful, and so _____ God acceptably with reverence and awe, for our 'God is a consuming fire'" (Hebrews 12:27-29).

_____

_____

_____

Thinking of Others ...

Grace Giver, thank you! Thank you for the grace in our lives. You give us a vision, a thought, a hope, a person to hold on to during our valleys and even on our mountaintop experiences. We find thankfulness in just being — being in your presence.

_____

_____

_____

Repentance ...

Life Giver, I thank you for the air I breathe, the lungs you gave me, the heart you designed in me, and just for the significance of thankfulness. I can't be happier than when I am truly grateful for wherever I am. Father, please forgive me for overlooking your sovereign insight of where I am today, because I know tomorrow is just a fulfillment of what you have shown me today. God, I fail to remember, quite often, how much you have done for me. I have my little pity parties, but God, you're amazing! Thank you!

_____

_____

_____

My Desires ...

"Thank you for loving and setting me free; thank you for giving your life just for me. Oh, how I thank you, gratefully thank, you, Jesus I thank you, and I thank you, thank you, Lord." That song runs through my mind over and over again. I guess the reason why is, God, I want you to know that my thankfulness comes from within.

_____

_____

_____

What are you thankful for? Even if it's for the dust on your feet because that means you have been somewhere, thank him!

Day #23:
SINGING A SONG ALL DAY LONG

The Sense of Humor Spot:

A man was wandering in the woods, pondering all the mysteries of life and his own personal problems. The man couldn't find the answers, so he sought help from God.

"God? You there, God?" he asked.

"Yes. What is it, my son?" God answered.

"Mind if I ask a few questions?" the man asked.

"Go ahead, my son, anything."

"God, what is a million years to you?"

God answered, "A million years to me is only a second."

The man asked, "God, what is a million dollars worth to you? "

God replied, "A million dollars to me is worth only a penny."

The man lifted his eyebrows and asked his final question. "God, can I have a penny?"

God answered, "Sure, give me a second."

WORD

There is something about praising God, praising others, telling about the goodness around us all day long that brings me the most joy. It is learning to have a heart of worship.

Most of the time, we think of worship as singing in a group at church. I believe it's life's challenges that teach us how to worship. The obstacles I have faced, the happiness from the natural experiences of just plain ol' living, the storms of life, as well as the gift of the rainbow experiences, have all taught me the heart of worship.

The purpose of our worship is to glorify, honor, praise, exalt, and please God. With all that being said, worship can happen all day long. It doesn't have to be contained inside a place with walls that we call a "church." We were meant to glorify, honor, praise, exalt, and please God all day long in our houses, cars, at football games, shopping — everywhere we are. Worship goes with us to all those places because worship is what comes out of our heart.

Whether life is giving or taking away, we can praise him. Even in the storms, we can know there is a Shelter. The clouds (the hurt, depression, sadness), the winds (the anger, the quarrels), and the elements of this season (whether you are feeling like you're on top of the world or in a deep, dark pit) will change. No matter what season of life you are in, if the sun is shining and you see the radiant flower, or all you see is gray skies, clouds, no leaves on the trees, those different seasons are opportunities to worship. Worshipping throughout those seasons will renew your soul.

Come with me to Song of Solomon 1:4

(The word Solomon means "peace.")

Take me away with you How many times I have wanted to be taken away from a situation by God? **let us hurry!** taken away in a hurry, I might add. **Let the king bring me into his chambers.** I want to be in God's presence. **We rejoice and delight in you;** There is something about just enjoying who God is, giving him praise, and just taking pleasure in him that make me want to sing. **We will praise your love more than wine.** When you celebrate love by giving love, receiving love, just enjoying the pleasure of love, it is more invigorating, cheering, and intoxicating than wine. **How right they are to adore you!** Adoring Jesus is so right!

What I learned:

The next time you feel an urge to kick something, sing! The next time you feel the urge to scream, sing! The next time your husband can't find his socks that are in his sock drawer, or your kids won't put their socks in their drawer, sing! Sing because it brings peace. Praise God in the joys of life and in the depths of the ditches that this life will bring. Sing! I have seen this over and over again in my life.

I love to dance. I think down deep inside us everyone wants to dance, but that ol' silly pride kicks in. Have you ever observed kids and adults at weddings? When the dancing first starts, everyone is timid, with the exception of someone like me, but little by little, the floor becomes full of dancers of all shapes and sizes. The one thing I see in all of them is joy, a smile, a love for life. In that moment, they put away the things in their lives that cause them to "think too much," and they dance.

Worship can happen in many forms: singing, dancing, speaking words of encouragement, smiling, and loving. It's in the doing of those things that we become free!

Your turn in the Word:

"Come, let us _____ for joy to the LORD; let us shout aloud to the Rock of our salvation. Let us come before him with _____ and extol him with _____ and song. For the LORD is the _____ God, the _____ King above all gods" (Psalm 95:1-3).

_____

_____

_____

Thinking of Others ...

Song of our heart, Jesus, that is what you are: a song we want to sing. You are love. Father, please rain down songs of your merciful love on each and every one of us. Give us a heart of worship, even if we are knee deep in dirt or flying high in the sky. But especially let us sing in the day-in-and-day-out of just living.

_____

_____

_____

Repentance ...

Song Giver, You know that I have sung songs that sounded like the biggest pity party ever thrown. I worshipped in ways that have not been pleasing to you. I have even squashed the joy of life because I decided to whine instead of sing. I will sing a new song to you.

_____

_____

_____

My Desires ...

OK, this desire is a really good desire, but it may be my desire and not yours, so here it goes: God, I just want to sing like Carrie Underwood. OK, so that is a selfish desire, but I do ask that when I sing, whether in song, words, or in showing love, that it will be pleasing to you.

_____

_____

_____

Today you should just try it. What song will you sing, what act of worship or love will you give to another?

I am going to dance today. That's right, dance! It may be in my bathroom, but this sista' is going to bust a move! How about you?

Day #24:
IT'S NOT ABOUT THE
THING, its about the relationship

The Sense of Humor Spot:

A burglar broke into a home and was looking around. He heard a soft voice say, "Jesus is watching you." Thinking it was just his imagination, he continued his search. Again the voice said, "Jesus is watching you." He turned his flashlight around and saw a parrot in a cage. He asked the parrot if he was the one talking and the parrot said, "Yes." He asked the

parrot what his name was and the parrot said, "Moses." The burglar asked, "What kind of people would name a parrot Moses?"

The parrot said, "The same kind of people who would name their pit bull Jesus."

WORD

Have you or are you addicted to something or someone? Have you or are you in a place where you're thinking you won't get over it or them? Have you ever seen something that seemed like a black and white decision or choice at one point in your life, but soon those choices turned gray?

I had a very wise man counsel me when I asked him about pursuing a choice that was gray. He said, "The very fact that it is gray is a warning that something is not right." Have you created a relationship with a person or a thing that you are not sure about? Is it gray? Get back to the basics of truth by going for the black/white answer. It should be clear.

See, God is not worried about the thing or the person; he is concerned more about your relationship with it or them. You will always know in your heart because it causes dis-ease. This thing or person will take up time that you know should be spent somewhere else. The reason this dis-ease is there is really a gift. It's kind of like your dashboard. It will flash a red seat belt sign until you put your seat belt on. It can be so annoying, but you know it's the right thing. As soon as you put your seat belt on, the flashing red sign goes away, and then there is a deep down sense of peace because you did the right thing. You really should've put on the seat belt in the first place.

It's the same concept with relationships that become unhealthy. There will be flashing red lights all around you that are brighter and louder than fireworks on a black night. For example, what if family members and friends warn you about the person you should get away from? You might think they are trying to take away your fun or they don't understand. You think, "If they only knew them." But remember, in the dashboard of your life, your family and friends can sometimes alert you to danger. They just want to protect you like your seatbelt.

Then there are the things we purchase that we know we can't afford or that we can't stop consuming — too much food, drinks, drugs, medications, or even a relationship that is out of balance. You will feel the flashing red light of dis-ease. From that point on, it's a decision, a choice you are faced with. Am I going to choose life or death? When you choose life, it will be tough because your flesh will want to fight it like crazy. But your heart will know it's right. If you choose death, whatever choices you are making now might not be flashing big bright red lights (signs of death), but tomorrow after dating the person who seemed to be a gray area, you might end up with a broken marriage, a sick body, or behaviors you wish you hadn't done. I wish I could sugarcoat this for us, but it is what it is.

God knows we will fight those red lights all our lives, and he understood that from the beginning. He is not as much concerned, I believe, with the red light issues as he is concerned with our relationship with him being first in our lives. As we have a relationship with him and love him with all our hearts and minds, those red lights seem to not appear as much because we begin to get out of the driver's seat and let him do the driving and the decision making. As we begin to understand what it is to love others as ourselves (and that comes from studying the word to get a healthy view of ourselves), then we begin to have less dis-ease because we understand how to have green light relationships that are based on God's way and not our own ways.

Come with me to Psalm 41:7-8

All my enemies Your enemies are your red lights. **whisper together against me; they imagine the worst for me, saying, "A vile disease** The Strong's Concordance says this of the word disease, "a matter or thing, act, affair, deed, effect, judgment, language, lying, message, effect, harm, hurt, portion, promise, sentence, sign, thought, work, word." **has beset him; he will never get up from the place where he lies."** Your enemies (red lights) want to keep you from getting up. They want to keep you bound, down, and dependent. Stress is a big red light!

What I learned:

God is not worried so much about your "issue" as he is the relationship you have with those issues. He wants us to love all of him, more than anything else. When that is in balance and you are walking in a healthy relationship with yourself and others, and when you are loving others as yourself, then those "issues" become less and he becomes more. It is hard to fight your flesh because it wants everything right now, but wisdom knows what you should do deep in your heart and leads you to do it.

Your turn in the Word:

"Do not love the _____ or anything in the _____. If anyone loves the _____, the love of the Father is not in him. For everything in the _____ — the cravings of sinful man, the lust of his eyes, and the boasting of what he has and does — come not from the Father but from the _____. The _____ and its desires pass away, but the man who does the will of God lives forever" (I John 2:15-17).

_____

_____

_____

Thinking of Others ...

Healer, heal our hearts. Give us the desire to want to see, listen, and obey. When we see a red light in our life, help us to stop, turn, and go the other direction, immediately. Please, God, let us be so filled with you that we choose to do life your way and not the world's way.

_____

_____

_____

Repentance ...

Father of Truth, I have gone right through the red lights in my life, and after doing so, I felt this tremendous guilt. Sometimes I even saw another red right light and continued to do it anyway. Please, God, forgive me for my willful disobedience.

_____

_____

_____

My Desires ...

Peace of God, give me the desire to stop at the red lights that I see ahead and make a right choice to turn into your ways. Let me hate any desire to run those red lights (lust of the flesh, lust of the eyes, or boastful pride) and let me live forever by doing your will.

_____

_____

_____

What is your mind set on? What are the red lights in your life? You know deep down that God and family are warning you to turn the other way.

Turning away from what we think we want is one of the hardest things to do. Ask God for help, pray, obey, and if you need to, find a friend who can truly understand your struggle, and will help you through prayer to overcome.

Day #25:
DOING THE MATH

The Sense of Humor Spot:
A little boy was waiting for his mother to come out of the grocery store. As he waited, he was approached by a man who asked, "Son, can you tell me where the post office is?"

The little boy replied, "Sure! Just go straight down this street a couple of blocks and turn to your right."

The man said, "Thank you, kindly; I'm the new pastor in town. I'd like for you to come to church on Sunday. I'll show you how to get to Heaven."

SURE, JUST GO DOWN THIS STREET A COUPLE OF BLOCKS AND TURN TO YOUR RIGHT

The little boy replied with a chuckle. "Awww, come on. You don't even know the way to the post office."

WORD

1 + 1 = 2, right? A song in the concordance is defined as a "metrical composition." We use math in music, in athletics, in cooking, in measuring our supplies or chemicals, in our finances, in our emotional tank, in our eating and calorie intake, and in our time. Math is a big part of our lives. We use it every day. I remember being in high school in geometry and thinking, "When am I going to ever use this?"

I may not use a ton of geometry every day, but there is a purpose and a plan for everything. I can clearly see 1 + 1 = 2. There are times when life is really that simple, but I complicate it. It's just what I do, especially when my emotions or my physical wants are screaming out, and I end up with a -2. When I withdraw from doing the right thing and choose to do my thing, I end up withdrawing too much, and I am left with a negative, a void, emptiness. Life is truly about balance. Life is life. All around you are TOO many choices. So much good, yet so much evil. We can't run from that truth, so we need to learn how to find balance and moderation in the life we live. How? Do the math.

Before I make a decision, I have to ask myself, "Will this choice bring life or death? Will this decision be in the best interest of everyone involved? What does the Bible have to say about this?"

Wisdom is knowing what to do and doing it. Basically, knowing 1 + 1 = 2. For example, if I buy this, it will drain my bank account, or if I eat that whole cake (and not just a piece) my bootie is going to grow. One more example — if I plant a tomato plant, I am not going to get corn. OK, just one more. If I reject or disrespect my husband, I will withdraw from our emotional "bank" account. It all adds up or subtracts. Math doesn't lie. It is what it is.

COME WITH ME TO PROVERBS 3:21-22

My son or daughter, **preserve** guard **sound judgment** clear thinking **and discernment;** common sense **do not let them out of your sight;** I don't know about you, but sometimes I don't want to use clear thinking or common sense because I want it my way. **they will be life for you,** When I don't use clear thinking and common sense, it usually brings about some kind of disappointment in myself. But when I do use clear thinking and common sense, I have a sense of goodness, and I hold my head up high. **an ornament to grace your neck.**

What I Learned:

As simple as $1 + 1 = 2$, that is how simple it is to see truth. I (the complicator) complicate things by adding to the equation of my life things that won't and don't fit. When I use clear thinking and common sense, the math of my life usually adds up, and I live a balanced life. It is when I try to fit my wants, mentally, physically, and emotionally, into something that God does not have planned for me, that is when I get in trouble.

My mental, physical, and emotional accounts have negative withdrawals, but, that's a big but, God can restore me no matter how much of a mess I have gotten myself into. He can take me from the biggest pit to a palace, if, and only if, I am willing to do the simple math of his principles, his ways, and live my life for him.

Your Turn in the Word:

"Do not forsake _____, and she will protect you; love her, and she will watch over you. Wisdom is supreme; therefore _____ wisdom. Though it _____ all you have, get understanding" (Proverbs 4:6-7).

_____

_____

_____

Thinking of Others...

Spirit of the Living God, do only what you can do. Speak to each one of my family members and friends in the area they need you right now. God, give them the desire to want to "look at the numbers," "do the math," and gain understanding from you. Each one of them is unique, and they need you in different ways. Speak specifically to them in your perfect timing. Thank you for your faithfulness.

_____

_____

_____

Repentance ...

Oh, Lord, my God, I have left clear thinking and common sense behind so many times so that I could go my foolish ways. Father, I need you. I need your presence moment by moment to help me want to do the math. By making common sense choices, day by day, and living to please you, the math of my life will add up.

_____

_____

_____

My Desires ...

Master of my mind, I want to be a math genius of clear thinking and common sense. I want to do immediately what I know to do when I hear it, not when I feel like it. God, I desire to apply your equations for my life and to run from mine that won't ever add up the way you or I want them to.

_____

_____

_____

What equation of your life doesn't have balance or isn't adding up? Ask God to give you the right heart to make those equations work out! He is faithful! Prayer is power! No prayer, no power!

Day #26:
HEart

The Sense of Humor Spot:
The top nine ways to know if you have PMS:
9. Everyone around you has an attitude problem.
8. You're adding chocolate chips to your cheese omelet
7. The dryer has shrunk every last pair of your jeans.
6. Your husband is suddenly agreeing to everything you say.
5. Everyone's head looks like an invitation to batting practice.
4. You're convinced there's a God, and he's male.
3. You're counting down the days until menopause.

2. You're sure that everyone is scheming to drive you crazy.
1. The ibuprofen bottle is empty, and you bought it yesterday.

WORD

HEart ... I love this. I remember the day this word came into my life. It was Valentine's Day, and I was driving to pick up my youngest at her pre-school. My heart was tender with thankfulness and love as tears flowed down my cheeks from the emotions that were welling up inside me.

When I got to the parking lot, I put my car in park and sat there like a little baby giggling on the inside. On the outside, it looked like my world was crumbling, but on the inside, God was at work. At that moment, I realized how deep of a love God had for me — just the way I was and for who I was (created in his image, his likeness). My world would never be the same when this word came into my thoughts.

HEart ... HE is the art in my heart. He knows me like no other ever would because he was the artist of my canvas. He painted the personality I have. It will never ever be like anyone else. He painted every square inch of my physical body, knowing that with each thing I try to change (of his art), my heart will break. He painted me this way for many reasons, knowing my physical body would change in different seasons. He is the Master Painter. Why do I try to change what he created? He painted my colorful family and friends. I see the true beauty within. He created the moon and the stars. The ocean has never skipped a beat; it moves with grace, with every tide it seems to be OK with its place. The animals are never trying to change who God created them to be. They don't stand in front of mirrors picking themselves apart. They are just free, enjoying who God intended them to be.

As I went to pick up my little girl, I thought of all the ways I have tried to change his original masterpiece since I was her age. Too many to count. I wanted to change my brown eyes to blue. I wanted to have thick, long hair. I wanted to lengthen my thighs a million times. I wanted to be tall and tan. I wanted to never be sad, but instead to be a ball full of joy.

It was then I realized with each brush of "my stroke" of art, I was changing his original masterpiece into something I was never meant to be. He designed me perfectly for his plan, not mine. He is the art of my HEart. He knows all the plans, designs, and patterns for my life. Since that day, I have reached a new level, learning to trust him, do my best, and just rest in who he painted me to be and become.

Come with me to Luke 12:22 & Prov 31:30

Then Jesus said Jesus said this, I didn't. **to his disciples:** Disciples are those who learn and are a pupil of Jesus, yesterday and today. **"Therefore I tell you,** Are you someone who is learning from Jesus? Then this is for you and all who seek to learn about him. **do not worry** Don't be anxious or worry about a "thing" or seeking out your own interests! Seek out his interests for your life, your soul, every breath you take, seek him for guidance. **about your life, what you will eat;** When I seek him and do what I know to do, whether that is eat the banana and not the cake or stop at one serving instead of 10, then I won't need to be anxious. Trust me, I know how hard this is, and I can only be balanced in my life because of my relationship with Him. **or about your body,** The body is a tough thing in this world of perfection we live in. God never intended for us to be this self-absorbed with our outside appearance. God designed you and me specifically for the needs he has to fulfill his perfect will on this earth. I have to trust that what he has given me is designed by the Master, himself, who knew what every curve of my body's shape and what color every hair on my head would be, and it is exactly the way he designed it for his purpose. Only you can accept that. No one can accept that for you. **what you will wear."** In this fashion-frenzied world we live in, I know this is difficult. The deal is, try your best with what he gave you, and wherever you are, but don't put too much into it because... **"Charm is deceptive, and beauty is fleeting; but a woman who fears the Lord is to be praised."**

What I learned:

HEart ... He (God) is the artist of my heart. He designed the art in my heart and brushed every stroke to create his masterpiece. I, myself, am not saying I am a "masterpiece," but I know who God is, and I've discovered he doesn't make mistakes. Each one of us is his masterpiece.

I have finally learned to appreciate his unique piece of art in myself. No one will ever think exactly like me (Lord knows!), talk exactly like me, make decisions exactly like me, love like me, laugh like me, look like me, or have my personality — and he loves what he has created. I am criticizing him when I criticize myself in areas that he designed. It has taken me a long, long time to understand this truth. It is still a struggle at different seasons in my life to not want to change how he made me. Those are usually the days I am looking at too many advertisements, the presumably "perfect" people I see (nobody is perfect), to the things of this crazy world that say, "You're not enough." It's on those uncertain days of struggle that I look to him and say, "God, You know me; now help me to see myself the way you see me."

Luke 10:27 helps me with this. It says we are to "Love the Lord your God with all your heart and with all your soul and with all your strength and with all your mind" and to "Love your neighbor as yourself."

I am scared sometimes for my neighbor because I don't know about you, but I don't love myself too nicely sometimes ... (not in love with myself, but love and respect myself through thinking and knowing how to love myself the way God loves me and sees me). I have to read, understand, listen, and do what the scriptures in the Bible say so that I can truly love myself and follow that small, still voice speaking truth in my ears all day long.

Your turn in the Word:

"So God _____ man in his own image, in the image of God he created him; male and female He created them" (Genesis 1:27).

_____

_____

_____

Thinking of Others ...

God, your word is truth. In Genesis 1:27, you say we were created in your image, your likeness. So that means my friends reading this and I have to know you created us. In Genesis 1:31, it says you looked at what you created and said, "It is good." Father, teach us to love and appreciate every unique stroke you brushed our personality with, our physical characteristics from our head to our toes, simply our very beings. Let us look at what you created and say to ourselves, "It is good."

_____

_____

_____

Repentance ...

God, You are so amazing. I look at the mountains, the seas, the stars, the trees, the animals and all that you created. They don't spend their days trying to change their appearance. They just are! Father, I have hurt you, I know, by trying to change my core, my appearance, my personality, and so much more. You must've been hurt when I tried to undo each beautiful stroke of your unique Masterpiece. You are the art in my HEart, and I will see the beauty within and appreciate myself your way, not mine or any other person's.

_____

_____

_____

My Desires ...

Creator of my heart, you know me like no other ever will. I desire to truly see myself as you do, day in and day out. I know one thing is for certain, you never change. You will love me and the art you created in me every second of every day. Help me to do the same.

_____

_____

_____

If you could repaint a part of your personality, your body, or anything about yourself, what would it be? Write it down. You can't conquer what you can't confront.

Now, ask God, first, "Did you create this or did I?" Then ask Him to help you appreciate that part of yourself and not degrade it.

Ask Him to show you why you put so much into that one thing when there are so many other great things about you!

Day #27:
IT'S NOT THE PAINT
THAT makes a warrior!

The Sense of Humor Spot:

A couple of New Jersey hunters are out in the woods when one of them falls to the ground. He doesn't seem to be breathing; his eyes are rolled back in his head.

The other guy whips out his cell phone and calls the emergency services. He gasps to the operator: "My friend is dead! What can I do?"

117

The operator, in a calm, soothing voice, says: "Just take it easy. I can help. First, let's make sure he's dead."

There is a silence, then a shot is heard. The guy's voice comes back on the line. He says: "OK, now what?"

Word

Have you ever dressed up as something you really weren't? When I was in the 5th grade, I went to a private Christian school. Our team name was the "Warriors," and our mascot was a warrior. I always loved the name Warriors because it was strong and powerful! The definition of a warrior is a person engaged or experienced in warfare or a person engaged in some struggle or conflict. When my brothers would head out on the Warriors' football field, I would cheer so loud for them I would lose my voice. Every time game day came, they were in a battle on that field.

As any real warrior knows, the battle begins way before the battle-field. It begins in a place where no one is really watching except the coach (God) and the warrior. The practice field is where true warriors are developed. Warriors show up for practice, rain or shine, because they know they can grow inside and out from just being around and being influenced by the coach. Regardless of the weather, warriors pump some iron (build their muscles) and watch game video (look at what they did or the other team did so they can learn from their experiences). Warriors plan their positions and plays go over them again and again so that when the enemy attacks, they are prepared to fight.

Think about how scared a (football player) "warrior" would be if he never went to practice, never pumped iron, never learned plays, or listened to the coach. How comfortable do you think he would be suiting up in a "Warrior" football uniform on game day looking at athletes on the opposing team who were twice his size? (This was true for our Warrior team. We were a small team, except for my brothers, of course.) Would you be prepared to face an opposing team that had a record of 12 wins, no losses? It just wouldn't make sense. It's not what you paint the outside when everyone is watching; it's what's on the inside.

What have you been practicing day in and day out? What are you preparing for? I know for me, I suit up everyday for the field of this crazy life. In order for me to win the battle of the mind, body, and soul, I have to listen to my coach (God), learn from him, listen to his plays, work out my muscle of faith through trusting him, and take actions that will lead me to ...V-I-C-T-O-R-Y!

We use to have this cheer that went like this. You have to kinda sing it:

Stop, look, and listen, here come the mighty Warriors
Stop, look, and listen, here come the mighty Warriors ...
Stop ... look and listen!
Here they come!

Come with me to Matthew 23:25

Woe to you, teachers of the law and Pharisees, Pharisees were known as self-righteous and prideful. They looked like they were perfect to those around them, but their hearts were far from God. **you hypocrites! You clean the outside of the cup and dish,** Who wants to drink out of a cup that is gross on the inside? We are so focused on our outsides, but true happiness comes from what is inside our cups (hearts). **but inside they are full of greed and self-indulgence.**

What I learned:

It's not the paint that makes the warrior or the princess. Truly, how many times have I seen such a beautiful person on the outside be so conflicted on the inside? I, myself, have been that person at times, but thankfully I have always known the King of kings, my warrior "Coach."

I have learned to get understanding by reading his playbook, the Bible, and showing up to practice each day, rain or shine, to grow, build my faith muscle, take action, and build my relationship through prayer and conversation with the biggest, baddest warrior around, Jesus Christ. I have learned I can't just wear the cross and carry the Bible, but I have to constantly be cleaning the inside of my cup, not just the outside.

Your turn in the Word:

"Blind Pharisee! _____clean the _____of the cup and dish, and then the outside also will be_____" (Matthew 23:26).

_____

_____

Thinking of Others ...

Maker of our cups, thank you for making us inside and out. God, give us the wisdom to appreciate the way you made us, from the inside out. Father, let our insides be filled with you so our outsides are just a beautiful reflection of who you truly are.

_____

_____

_____

Repentance ...

Living and active God, your truth pierces my heart and penetrates any thoughts or attitudes I have. Lord, I am being delivered day by day from the deception of making my cup appear clean on the outside. I ask you to forgive me for the days that I fail to change what is going on inside and instead "fix up" the outside.

_____

_____

_____

My Desires ...

I want the squeakiest clean cup inside and out! I want to know you in a way that my cup overflows with all that you are: love, joy, peace, patience, kindness, goodness, faithfulness, gentleness, and self-control.

_____

_____

_____

OK, let's do our "Warrior Cheer"!
Stop ...
Look ...
Listen ...
Stop what you are doing, look, and now listen. What do you see and hear? What does your cup look like? What are you painting on the outside? Is there dirt on the inside?
Let's clean the inside of our cups and drink up his love!

Day #28:
COME AS A CHILD

The Sense of Humor Spot:
Good Ol' Redneck Saying:
"I don't play — I quit school 'cause of recess."

WORD

I love to watch children and nature. Why? Well, I am so glad you asked. They have something in common: They are natural; they just are who they are. Watch the way they play, so effortlessly, with imagination

and laughter. Listen to the way they communicate with one another. Observe how they come to you for all their needs, like a hug, some kisses, approval, attention, food, clothing, basic necessities, comfort, high-fives, and so, so much more. Watch how easily they forgive and forget.

I have seen a kid get smacked upside the head with a frying pan by his friend, and within minutes, they were on the floor playing Legos. I have seen sweet little girls say some of the meanest things to one another, and within an hour, they are pouring tea and sipping it together — little princesses in their royal palace deciding on their next imagination destination. Children are eager to learn, eager to laugh, eager to live, eager to love. How can children do that?

Children just are. They don't sit around worrying about too much. They just "eat the banana and throw out the peel." They eat the juicy wholeness of life and throw out the hard stuff. They are that simple. They don't build emotional cases against people. They don't judge based on appearances. If you give them positive attention, they think you are the coolest person they know. They forgive within a breath. Worries, if they have any, they will usually tell you and then move on for more playing and using their imaginations. They're not too worried about where they are going next, unless you have been in the car for more than one hour; then they want to know, "How much longer?" and "Where are we going again?"

Oh, to be a child again. Guess what?! I can, I think! Of course, I have to be an adult and make adult decisions all day long, but I sometimes forget how to use my imagination, laugh, forgive, and just play. I also find myself not as eager as a child, or I might find myself resisting learning something new ... heaven forbid, huh?

Each day I am learning how much fun life is when I choose to laugh, love, forgive, learn, grow as a child, and, most importantly, go to my Father for approval, love, comfort, high-fives, protection, provision, forgiveness, thankfulness, hugs, and kisses.

Come with me to Luke 9:47-48

Jesus, knowing their thoughts, Jesus knows our thoughts, too. He knows how competitive we are as adults. We all want to be the best, the greatest. He knows how hard it is for us to be truly humble. He also knows we know our background. He knows we feel insufficient and undeserving to be forgiven or to be loved unconditionally. He knows that; that is why he came to set you free from those things. We just have to come as children, simply believe, ask him to forgive us, and allow him to come into our lives. He loves us and wants us no matter what. He doesn't look back once we give our lives to him and trust him like a child! Simply believe! **took a little child and had him stand beside him.** Why do you think Jesus took a child and had the boy stand beside him? He wanted them to see how simple a child is in every aspect of life. He was also demonstrating how a child is the least (the littlest) in the "chain of command," if you will.

Then he said to them, "Whoever welcomes this little child in my name welcomes me; and whoever welcomes me welcomes the one who sent me. For he who is least among you all — he is the greatest." When we let go of who we are and humble ourselves to become more like Jesus, we become the greatest. But, not greatest in the world's view of greatest. Greatest, as in God's kingdom, which is everlasting, eternal, and definitely a place I want to be a part of.

What I Learned:

Life is simple. I am the one who complicates it! I am learning more and more every day by observing young children how to be a really cool adult. Not that I am really cool (yet, hopefully there will be a day), but young children are. They are free! They are not worried about "being the greatest," but they are just being who God created them to be: eager to love, eager to learn, eager to forgive, eager to give, eager to laugh, eager to play. (When was the last time you were eager to play ... and without being worried about winning, but just playing to be playing?).

They're eager to wake up in the morning because they get to eat pancakes with chocolate chip eyeballs, a strawberry nose, and whip cream lips in the morning and wear their favorite pants that are too short and covered in stains. They don't care, because that's them!

Your turn in the Word:

"I tell you the truth, anyone who will not receive the kingdom of God like a little _____ will never enter it" (Luke 18:17).

_____

_____

_____

Thinking of Others ...

Father, my friend reading this is your child. You designed this person to laugh the way they laugh, cry the way they cry, create the way they create, and love the way they love. Let them be free like a child to live all their lives like your child, trusting you for all their needs, provisions, protections, comforts and desires. Let them humble themselves to come to you as a child and become like you, great in God's kingdom that lasts forever.

_____

_____

_____

Repentance ...

Pure love, that is what you are Lord, pure. I have altered your pure child by going to the things of this world for comfort and protection. I need your forgiveness for not trusting you as a simple child would; rather, I have complicated my life by thinking I am a big girl, and I can do this life on my own. Lord, just as children need their parents every hour of every day, I need you just that way.

_____

_____

_____

My Desires ...

Sweet Daddy, I want to always come to your lap first, before I even think of going anywhere else for all my needs or wants. I want to please you first, just as my little girls want to please me. I want to be so connected to you moment by moment and talk to you about every decision, every thought, every action I am going to take or make and give it to you for guidance and celebration!

_____

_____

_____

What has you wound up tighter than a banjo string? When was the last time you just played, laughed more than once in a day, were eager to learn, or ate pancakes with chocolate eyeballs, a strawberry nose and whip cream? Think like a child; humble yourself as a child; be free!

Day #29: MICROWAVE ME, PLEASE!

The Sense of Humor Spot:

One school day I cut up some cantaloupe for my girls to eat when they got in the car after a long day of school. As the little one ate, she asked, "Mom, what animal do cantaloupes come from?"

I told her they came from the ground. She was insistent that they came from an animal. So finally it hit me, I said, "Do you mean antelopes?"

She replied with satisfaction and a smile, "Yeah, that's it! Cantaloupes come from antelopes."

WORD

Worry is like a rocking chair. I rock back and forth. Am I supposed to do this or do that? Should I let my kids go there? What if I lose that person in my life? What will happen if …? But I never really get anywhere. I just rock, back and forth. Worry — I spend way too much time being anxious rather than talking to or trusting the One who can help me with my rocking-chair worry. How about you?

I recently heard someone say "Worry means there is something in your life over which you cannot have your way!" Ouch! I guess when I don't get something I want in life, I end up being irritated with God, and that can't be good. Worry comes in so many forms and many times it is something we use to make others, and ourselves, think we are "really busy." But all along, we are just rockin'.

It reminds me of this story I have heard and read about many times. I will tell it in my version: There were two sisters named Martha and Mary. They were having Jesus and his disciples over for dinner. Martha was, well, a lot like Martha Stewart. She was busy making sure Jesus and his disciples had a comfortable cozy place to sit and a spread of food fit for kings. The candles were burning, and so was Martha, at both ends.

Mary, on the other hand, was just sitting at the feet of Jesus, listening to what he was saying and enjoying the relationship. I can just picture it. Martha, with her hand on her hip looking at Mary just "sitting" there, listening to Jesus. Then Martha complains to Jesus that Mary should be busy helping, but Jesus didn't give into Martha's victim mentality. He simply told her that "You are worried and anxious about many things, but only one thing is needed. Mary has chosen what is better, and it will not be taken away from her" (Luke 10:41-42). Now, I know that is not what Martha wanted to hear.

One thing that freed Mary from the busyness and worries experienced by her sister was that Mary chose to first focus on Jesus, listen to him and ignore the immediate demands of making the house look good, having everything prepared, and being hospitable. Mary wasn't being irresponsible, rather she wanted to experience a relationship and learn from Jesus first. Then later, when he was done speaking, she would fulfill her jobs around the house. Martha was doing good "things," but Mary's priority was Jesus — first.

From that story I learn that when I put God first, then he will free me from worries and take care of the rest of my concerns if (and only if) I give my concerns to him. Then I have to trust him to work everything out for good.

The worries of this world will choke out the life, the full and abundant life, we are intended to have. What causes you to worry? A few things that are written about the cause of worry are written in Mark 4:19, "… But the worries of this life, the deceitfulness of wealth, and the desires for other things come in and choke the word, making it unfruitful."

"The desires for other things" — maybe those are things we think we want, but not what God has planned for us.

Come with me to Luke 8:14

The seed The seed is the word of God. **that fell** To go down or descend into our hearts. **among thorns** The thorns represent hardness. Seeds need soil to grow in. **stands for those who hear, but as they go on their way,** As we live life, day in and day out. **they are choked** The words that give you life can be choked out and die. How? **by life's worries,** Life's worries are things that pertain to this earthly life. That is why you must also have eternity in mind every day of your life. **riches and pleasures,** Oh, the money and the fun. Those were things meant to give you abundant, peaceful lives, not out of control hurt, pain filled lives. **and they do not mature.** If we have no soil when we plant a seed (or the word of God), and all the words we hear that bring us life are just thrown on the thorny ways of our own free will, then we will never experience or be the full grown mature tree or person we were meant to be. We will just be prickly, with no leaves, no fruit, no shade, no protection — just hard!

What I learned:

The first step to overcome the anxieties and worries of this world is to cast your cares upon the Lord. Talk to God. Trust me, this relieves a ton of stress. Why? Because you are talking to THE ONE who made you. He who knew every worry you would have, every doubt, every fear (if you have kids, you have lots of those). You can't add a single hour to your life by worrying, so why do it?

The second step to overcome the anxieties and worries of your world is to ask yourself, "Could I possibly be chasing after something I want for myself, instead of what God wants for me?" and "Can I do anything positive about what I am worrying about? Do it! Sometimes, "giving it time," is the only positive thing you can do (see Isaiah 40:31).

Your turn in the Word:

"Cast _____ your _____ on Him because He cares for you" (1 Peter 5:7).

_____

_____

_____

Thinking of Others ...

Tree of life, you designed us to bear much fruit in our lives. We have a life full of worry without knowing you and your word (seeds) of truth. God, turn our thorny places into fertile soil. Let us be willing to absorb the moisture of your word daily so that we may be anxiety-free and full of all you meant for us to be.

_____

_____

Repentance ...

"Worry wart" — that's been me. You already know me, God. I have done such a great job of exercising my worry into full-blown distrust and anxiety. Jesus, I choose to leave my worries in my conversations with you and turn to completely trust you throughout my days, knowing you already have the answers. You are the truth, the way, and the light.

_____

_____

_____

My Desires ...

God, I really want a heart totally free from doubt, worry, and anxiety. I know I have learned how to do these negative, untrusting behaviors, so I can also learn how to change that doubt into trust, that worry into faith, and that anxiety into doing what I can do and leaving the rest up to you. Help me to do that very thing!

_____

_____

_____

List your top three worries:
1.
2.
3.

With each one, write how you will begin to trust God and do what you can do in each of those areas.

Sometimes worry is really full-blown procrastination.

We worry about a relationship — when we have the keys to re-open it or re-start it. We worry about our kids — when we could spend more time with them. We worry about our health — yet we sit on the couch and put no effort into helping our health,

And on, and on ....

If you can make a difference by taking action, just do it, and stop procrastinating!

Day #30:
SILENCE COMES BEFORE MUSIC

The Sense of Humor Spot:

Sherlock Holmes and Dr. Watson go on a camping trip. After a good dinner and a bottle of wine, they retire for the night and go to sleep. Some hours later, Holmes wakes up and nudges his faithful friend.

"Watson, look up at the sky and tell me what you see."

"I see millions and millions of stars, Holmes," replies Watson.

"And what do you deduce from that?"

Watson ponders for a minute. "Well, astronomically, it tells me that there are millions of galaxies and potentially billions of planets. Astrologically, I observe that Saturn is in Leo. Horologically, I deduce that the time is approximately a quarter past three. Meteorologically, I suspect that we will have a beautiful day tomorrow. Theologically, I can see that God is all-powerful and that we are a small and insignificant part of the universe. What does it tell you, Holmes?"

Holmes is silent for a moment. "Watson, you idiot!" he says. "Someone has stolen our tent!"

WORD

One of the greatest benefits from being in a church community is that you get to experience, see, and learn from one another's personal gifts. The husband and wife team teaching my girls in a Wednesday night choir class were not just your typical volunteers; they were professional musicians. As I sat back and listened, I was so impressed. There were two statements that were said a couple of times that I kept telling myself not to forget. One was, "Silence comes before music," and the other was, "The most important part of music is the beginning (alpha) and the end (omega)."

129

As I kept hearing these phrases over and over again, I started to think about how relevant it was to life and living life in step with the Holy Spirit. I have been told many times to just get silent before the Lord, especially in the mornings. When you shuffle the word silent around it spells listen. This is a very tough thing to do, for me anyway. It is kinda like that Wednesday night couple trying to get all those kids to be silent before the music. It takes time and discipline to really stop, listen, wait, be silent, and look for the Composer (God) to give you the signal to begin at the same time.

There are so many mornings that my mind has "music," or, I believe the right term would be my "noise," in it before my feet hit the floor. Noise is different than music. Music has a beginning and end — alpha and omega — a rhythm. There is something you must know with all your very being. God has already ordered your footsteps before the beginning of time. He has already decided your path. Your life has already been set in motion from beginning (alpha) to end (omega). He sets before you two choices: life or death. Now the part that is tough to hear: Your choices will either keep you on God's path of a blessed life or a life of destruction leading to death. Blessed in God's eyes means a kneeled life, a peaceful life — not so much about the external — but the internal. It's a life of humility and falling under the authority of Jesus Christ, King of kings. In our lives today, that is a very tough challenge, to go from emails to kneel-mails.

God is looking for those who are choosing humility, not ego. Believe me, keeping this truth in front of me daily is so vital to my choices. I believe it's in those morning times of just spending time in silence that your choices for the day become clear to you. What will bring you and others around you life or death? The music of your life will be so much more beautiful if you wait for the Composer of your life to direct you note by note, step by step, from beginning (alpha) to end (omega).

Come with Me to Deuteronomy 30:19

"I call heaven and earth to record this day against you, [that] I have set before you life [green, flowing, lively, active, reviving] and death [destruction], blessing and cursing; therefore, choose life, that both thou and thy seed [your children, moral quality] may live ..." (KJV).

What I Learned:

Silence comes before the music. When is the last time you just got silent and listened from the beginning (alpha) to the end (omega) of your day? For me, when I have my day written out (usually the night before is best), I wake up, grab my coffee, and I speak to God, saying, "This is my day from beginning to end. What will bring life and peace or destruction? What will bring me a sweet melody or just cause noise?"

It's easy to see what brings life and what brings destruction, but now the hard part is the choices I make for the day. It could be a choice in just simply the words I speak, or it could be a choice of going to do something I need to go do, instead of putting it off. It could be a choice in loving someone who seems unlovable to me. I do know that when I choose life I not only begin to 'feel' whole; I become whole. At the end of your day (omega), reflect back on all those choices, and if you choose life all day, think how much happier and healthier you would be. Not to mention the sleep you will get.

Your turn in the Word:

"The tongue has the power of _____ and _____ and those who _____ it will eat its fruit" (Proverbs 18:21).

_____

_____

_____

Thinking of Others ...

Great Redeemer, I pray over choices my loved ones will make. Father, let them see your truth of life and give them the desire to choose life. You, great and all knowing God, have already ordered their steps; let them choose to walk in step with the Holy Spirit daily.

_____

_____

_____

Repentance ...

Prince of Peace, my words and choices don't match up at times. My words bring life, but my choices bring death. Father, please forgive my stubborn will, my selfish ways, and my evil desires.

_____

_____

_____

My Desires ...

Alpha and Omega, you are all-knowing of my beginning and my end. You are so gracious to set before me free will and choice. You are a gentleman and will not force your will on me, but you offer me peace, blessings, and life. God, teach me self-control so I may walk in true life. I choose you to love more than anyone else or anything else.

_____

_____

_____

Set your alarm early.
Get your coffee.
Look at your list for the day.
Pray
No Prayer = No Power
Silent? Listen at the alpha (beginning of your day) and the omega (end of your day).
What brings life? What brings destruction?

Day #31:
THE CONTENTS OF MY HEART

The Sense of Humor Spot:

"Everyone should have kids. They are the greatest joy in the world. But they are also terrorists. You'll realize this as soon as they are born, and they start using sleep deprivation to break you."

— Ray Romano

WORD

What is really in our hearts? While writing this book, I kept asking my friend what fonts I should use and what format I should put it in because I wanted it to be cute, and I wanted the cover to be awesome. Needless to say, I love to dress things up, decorate, and make everything I do look good. I am a retired hairdresser — what can I say? It's just in me to want to make the outside of everyone and everything look its best.

Her answer to me was, "Don't worry about the outside; just worry about the content."

That statement really got me thinking about the "inside" of this book and the contents of my heart. So I decided to look up the word *content* in the Webster's Unabridged Dictionary. Here is what *content* means, "That which is contained; the thing or things held by a receptacle or included within specified limits; as, the contents of a room; the contents of a book."

The English language is a beautiful thing, although confusing at times. Words can be spelled one way and pronounced a totally different way. Some words can be used as two different parts of speech. For example, the word CON-tent (accent on first syllable) or con-TENT (accent on second syllable.) I can talk about the CONtents of this book (which, by the way, is the contents of my heart), but the second way to pronounce that word is conTENT would mean to satisfy the desires of; to make easy in any situation; to appease or quiet; to gratify; to please; rest or quietness of the mind in one's present condition; freedom from discontent; satisfaction; contentment; moderate happiness.

If my heart has the right CONtents — that is to say, if I am filling my heart with truth, hope, love, joy — then my result will be that I am conTENT (restful or quiet of mind, freedom from discontent; satisfaction).

COME WITH ME TO I SAMUEL 16:7

But the Lord said to Samuel, "Do not consider his appearance or his height, Wow, this hit me. God's ways are not our ways for sure because we do put so much on appearances. **for I have rejected him. The Lord does not look at the things man looks at.** To be like God, you have to think like God. **Man looks with the physical eye at the outward appearance, but the Lord looks** to see, observe, consider, look at, give attention to, discern, distinguish **at the heart."** soul, heart (of man), mind, knowledge, thinking, reflection, memory, inclination, resolution, determination (of will), conscience, heart (of moral character).

WHAT I LEARNED:

So many times, I have been so concerned with what's going on outside myself — with situations and relationships — without examining the contents of my heart. I am so quick to see what I see with my physical eyes, yet when I dig deep and look into my spirit, I am quick to see not what man sees, but what the Lord sees.

God is so faithful to "shine his light" or point out when my heart is in need of something internally, not externally. I have to slow down and examine the contents of my heart, and if I am not content or restful, I know God is shining his bright light of truth on the contents of my heart.

YOUR TURN IN THE WORD:

"But the things that come out of the mouth come from the _____, and these make a man 'unclean'" (Matthew 15:18).

_____

_____

_____

Thinking of Others ...

Savior, save us from the contents of our hearts. Wash us clean. Lord, let each one of us be pure in heart by filtering what we fill the contents of our hearts with. Let us be on guard and seek out only truth, so we will be filled with contentment and rest.

_____

_____

_____

Repentance ...

Light of the world, your light shines brightly on the contents of my heart. I feel the heat of your refining fire on my issues. Father, I run to you to ask for your forgiveness for making my exterior appear like I am totally following you when I am really not. My heart contains unresolved issues that I know you are shining your truth on. Please forgive me for my short-comings in these areas and help me to want a pure heart more than anything else. I know it's only through you that this can be done. Help my faith and my actions to work in unity.

_____

_____

_____

My Desires ...

Savior, purify my heart, my mind, my will, my knowledge, and my conscience. God, I long to do what I know I should do. Give me your desires. I want to think like you think and then do what I know to do. Don't let go of me.

_____

_____

_____

Take one day, set it aside. Don't look in the reflection of a mirror, only reflect on your heart, your thoughts, your mind, your conscience, your knowledge, and your determinations. What is God shining his bright light on? What can you DO to put your faith in full motion toward changing that situation, relationship, thought, or your will? The first thing I am going to do is pray and act on what he sheds light on.

I'm praying for you!

Day #32:
IT'S THE WHY OF CONDITIONING

The Sense of Humor Spot:

Why can't women put on mascara with their mouths closed?

Why is 'abbreviated' such a long word?

Why is a boxing ring square?

Why is it called lipstick if you can still move your lips after you use it?

Why is what doctors do called "practice"?

Why is it that rain drops, but snow falls?

Why is lemon juice made with artificial flavor, and why is dishwashing liquid made with real lemons?

Why is the third hand on a watch called a second hand?

WORD

Understanding the why (for what reason, cause, or purpose) changes everything, yet nothing.

We were at basketball practice, and we love basketball. After a long, hard practice the coach looked at the girls and said, "Run laps." He gave no reason, no why, no nonsense. Just run. You should have seen the look on the girls' faces as they came around in the process of doing their laps. They looked confused, like they thought they practiced their hardest. Then there were the girls whose faces looked down right ticked. After they completed their laps, the coach asked, "Do you know why I made you run those laps?"

One girl, with a slight smile (probably thinking to herself, "I sure don't want to get in trouble for saying this.") said aloud, "Because you're mean?"

The coach laughed and began to explain that the purpose or "the why" was to condition their bodies and get them strong so they could endure the games. You see, the coach saw the big picture and didn't want the girls to get in the game and be totally defeated because he failed to prepare them. As soon as the girls understood "the why" of conditioning, they gladly ran laps at the next practice. They ran with intention and determination, each wanting to be the first one to finish.

The first time they ran the laps, they ran with doubt, questioning why in the world they had to run laps, but then they took time to listen to the coach and gained understanding of the why. Nothing really changed, but their perspective had changed!

Knowing the why: It doesn't excuse anything, but it sure can give you some insight when you know "the reason." Here are just a few examples that got me going on this:

There was a man who was in a store checking out with his three kids. These kids really weren't listening to him. With each request the man gave, the children seemed to not even respond. The clerk had already "decided" (judged) that this man needed to control his kids better and that he wasn't a good dad. As the dad placed his merchandise on the counter and began to pull out his wallet, he apologized to the clerk, "I am so sorry for my kids' behavior. Their mom just passed away and I work full time. Now I am a full-time father with a full-time job, and I'm not doing a good job at either right now."

The clerk immediately changed her tune. This "bad dad" was instantly "superman," and her feelings switched from critical to a deep sorrow for him and his loss. Nothing really changed. The "why" just showed up, and immediately the clerk had compassion.

If we knew why people did or didn't do what "we think" they should do, and we took the time out to find out the "why" behind it, our thought process quite possibly would change. Another reason why "the why" is so important is stated in scripture: "for lack of knowledge my people perish."

Here is another example. I've heard this story many times, but it is a great reminder to me to find out "the why":

A sweet, newly married young girl was cooking for her new in-laws and her family as well. She prepared a beautiful meal with ham, green bean casserole, cranberry sauce, and freshly baked rolls. As the family gathered around to eat, her mother-in-law noticed that both ends of the ham were cut off. She asked her precious new daughter-in-law, "Why are the ends of your ham cut off?" She said, "My grandma always did that, so that's what I do."

The mother-in-law was puzzled as to what would provoke a woman to cut off perfectly good meat. As they sat around the table, the girl's grandma explained, "I cut off the ends because my pan wasn't big enough for the whole ham." The whole table just laughed and laughed. Understanding "the why" would've provided the family with more meat and saved the new bride a lot of heckling from then on at family dinners. She just cut the ends off because it was what she learned, but she never asked "the why." This story clearly shows that asking "the why" gives understanding.

Another great example: I have girls, and we all know how tough girls can be to figure out, because for us females, what we mean and what we say are two different things. I've decided my girls are peacemakers. One of the little ladies was having one of those days. You know, one of those days where nothing I said she went with, every move was opposite from her natural self. She was in opposition. It stuck out like a sore thumb. Thank God for my days of listening to wiser women and men who taught me that when someone is acting out of character and is easily bothered, they are dealing with something that maybe they haven't even put their finger on. But something is restless and causing dis-ease.

On this occasion, I decided to slow the bus down and get off for a few stops, if you know what I mean. Life can get so busy that we forget to stop and find out "the why." Enough was enough, so I asked her to take a break, go to her room, and think about why she was acting out this way. Figuring out the why can solve so many miscommunications between husband/wife relationships, parent and kids, friends and foes. Knowing why is so revealing.

At this time I really didn't know what to do, because Lord knows I am no counselor, but I knew I could call on the Counselor. So I went into the bathroom and prayed. We always have handy little books that speak life into our lives in the bathroom. (Those books are one of my secret weapons!) So, motivated to go and truly listen to her day and her thoughts, I helped her get to the bottom of her behavior. When she finally landed the plane (found the root of the problem) after circling the runway (finding all the weeds, but not the root of the problem) for a good 10 minutes, we found out she needed time alone.

Life gets out of control sometimes, and we all need time to be alone. Something so simple could've gotten way out of hand had we not found out "the why."

Come with me to Psalm 49:2-3

Both low and high, Everyone has a deep need to be understood. **rich and poor alike:** No matter what your status, we all have this desire to be understood. If we would all just take time to understand one another's why. **My mouth will speak words of wisdom; the utterance from my heart will give understanding.** When you really listen to a person's words, it is like being able to look into a window of their heart and gain understanding of why they do what they do.

What I learned:

Taking time to stop, look, and listen to the why of someone's behavior will bring a clearer understanding of where their actions are coming from. When is the last time you stopped to ask yourself, I wonder what the why is behind my actions? I want to know why my family member is acting out in this way. We will all grow from gaining the "why" knowledge.

Your turn in the Word:

"In _____ we have redemption through his blood, the forgiveness of sins, in accordance with the riches of God's grace that _____ lavished on us with all wisdom and _____. And he made known to us the mystery of _____ will according to _____ good pleasure, which he purposed in Christ" (Ephesians 1:7-9).

_____

_____

_____

Thinking of Others ...

You, God, are Alpha and Omega. You know the beginning from the end and everything in between. Help us to want to understand the why of our behavior and others' actions. Help us to have complete compassion and patience to want to know the 'why' instead of judging others. Let us just simply love ourselves and others right where they are, unconditionally.

_____

_____

_____

Repentance ...

Father of truth, I cannot lie, nor do I want to. I want to completely confess and forsake any sin of judgment that I have ever made on anyone. Forgive me for not reaching out to understand the why of my own and others' sins.

_____

_____

_____

My Desires ...

God of mercy, I want to be so in tune with you and the way you give such understanding, even when we don't deserve it. You understand our whys, yet still invite us to have a real relationship with you, right where we are. Please, Father, let me be this unconditional and understanding of others' whys and even my own.

_____

_____

_____

What is something you can ask yourself today, "Why would _____ be doing this? What is the need that needs to be filled?" Ask God to show you the why of what you are doing, right now, today.

Day #33:
SEASONS OF CHANGE

The Sense of Humor Spot:
> Signs that you drink too much coffee:
>> You answer the door before people knock.
>> You ski uphill.
>> You grind your coffee beans in your mouth.
>> You haven't blinked since the last lunar eclipse.

You're the employee of the month at the local coffeehouse and you don't even work there.
Your eyes stay open when you sneeze.
You chew on other people's fingernails.
You can type sixty words per minute ... with your feet.
You can jump-start your car without cables.
You don't need a hammer to pound nails.
Your only source of nutrition comes from Sweet & Low.
You don't sweat, you percolate.

WORD

We are all experiencing a change in season. As I write this, the trees are dancing (as my little girl says), the leaves are beginning to fall, and we're starting to wonder what to wear ... flip flops, rain boots, or good ol' boots?

Perhaps you remember being a 5-year-old going to school for the first time, or perhaps you can remember walking through the cafeteria in junior high and bracing your tray, hoping someone would ask you to join them for lunch, and hoping you will actually make it there without tripping, only to lose all your food and that little bit of hope.

Maybe you're in college, grocery shopping at the deli for the first time (I mean, come on ... "How many pounds? What kind? What slice? Why do I feel so much pressure with all these people behind me?"). Or maybe your kids are heading off to college? Or perhaps you are losing something (a marriage, a job, finances, friendships, appearances) or worse, someone.

Change ... why do we embrace it or deny it? Why? Because, it's change! Change has brought many opportunities and much opposition to my life. I believe each season of our lives, whether we're selfish or we're serving; both are good, but both have to be balanced. Herein, we can learn life's lessons if we are looking for them.

In my life, changes in season have often excited me. For instance, the cool breeze at a high school football game. Unfortunately, not all days feel that invigorating, and it's on those days when I'm not feeling the cool breeze that I have to ask myself, "What's the lesson?" When life happens and my kids go left, but I take a right, or my health fails me, my family divides, my finances aren't adding up, my dog just threw up, and the very person I put total trust in fails me? What's the life lesson?

If I am a big enough girl, I can always learn something. Most of the time, it's a big lesson in a small circumstance, or it could be a big circumstance and a small lesson.

One day I was walking into my daughter's elementary school on the date of September 11, thinking, "I am just so thankful of where I am at this moment." I am.

See, I am a mom (alive and well), that's all, no titles, no letters behind my last name, just a girl with a family doing the best I can today. That simple. It hasn't always been that simple for me, I assure you. Lots of seasons have come and gone: an uncertainty of what I wanted to be when I grew up, but then I learned to find my passion. A season of loneliness, and then my husband Lin came along. A season of a love, a year of marriage, and then a season of counseling. A beautiful baby girl, and then two. Worrying about the size of my booty, a life altering dis-ease that brought me back to reality, and now humility.

You see, I've been up, I've been down, and in between, but I realize that seasons will come and go; changes will ensue. The difference is that now I ask myself, simply, "What is the lesson, how can I grow, and who can I serve today?" Just simple little me.

As I wrote that last question, I realize some of you are on top of the world, others in between, and then some of you are fighting to stay alive. As Rick Warren says in his book, *The Purpose-Driven Life*, "Real servants don't try to use God for their purposes. They let God use them for his purpose."

With change comes growth, and as your youngster can't keep the same pair of shoes for a whole year, so it is in the spiritual. Sometimes you have to just walk through one season to get to another. Change can be beautiful and painful, but know for sure that it's in the valley where we change and learn the most.

Come with me to Ecclesiastes 3:1-8

There is a time for everything, and a season for every activity under heaven: a time to be born and a time to die, a time to plant and a time to uproot, a time to kill and a time to heal, a time to tear down and a time to build, a time to weep and a time to laugh, a time to mourn and a time to dance, a time to scatter stones and a time to gather them, a time to embrace and a time to refrain, a time to search and a time to give up, a time to keep and a time to throw away, a time to tear and a time to mend, a time to be silent and a time to speak, a time to love and a time to hate, a time for war and a time for peace. Enough said!

W*hat* I l*ea*rn*e*d:

God is a God of seasons. He knows just what seasons to take us through that will draw us closer to Him. He is a God of timing. We get to choose how we go through the different seasons. Sometimes we create seasons for ourselves (God allows them), and other times God may give us a season so that we can recognize just how amazing he is, and how he just longs for us to totally trust him through each one.

Y*our* t*u*rn *i*n th*e* W*ord*:

"I know that _____ God does will endure forever; nothing can be added to it, and nothing taken from it. God does it so that men will _____ him" (Ecclesiastes 3:14).

_____

_____

_____

Thinking of Others ...

Because your love is better than life, we will choose to look to you for guidance, comfort, and hope in the midst of our circumstances. God, please let my loved ones feel your presence during the variety of experiences that they face in this beautiful process we call life.

_____

_____

_____

Repentance ...

Lord, my lips will glorify you during each change of season that will come and go in my life. Father, I have failed many times at totally trusting you during the uncertain times in my life. I will turn to you, faithful Friend, no matter what the seasons bring.

_____

_____

_____

My Desires ...

God, you are truly amazing! Really! I mean look at the way you planned all the different seasons in nature. You knew your trees needed to release the old leaves in the fall, rest during the winter, bud in the spring, and provide shade in the summer. Only you could be that detailed. I love that about you! Lord, I want to see each season as a time of growth even when it feels like I am dying. Without a doubt, in my fall and winter seasons, I want to be so sure of the bud and growth that are coming!

_____

_____

_____

What season are you in? Do you feel like you are losing some old leaves, dying completely, budding, or are you in full growth?

What are you learning about your relationship with God during this season?

Day #34:
IF I HAD NO TOMORROW

The Sense of Humor Spot:
"If your parents never had children, chances are, you won't either."
— Dick Cavett

MY PARENTS NEVER HAD CHiLDREN

WORD

Have you ever been so mad at someone close to you? A "someone" you will never be totally disconnected from because they are family? I guess you could disconnect yourself, but let's just say this "someone" is a person you choose to always be connected to.

Take my husband, for instance. First of all, we have two wedding bands and one commitment ... our two hearts were joined as one when we said "I do." Secondly, we have two beautiful daughters that weave our lives together even tighter. All that to say, my man is someone I will always be connected to. No matter what this whirlwind of life brings, we will be connected.

Now, as all of you know, whether you're married or not, relationships are tough. But so rewarding! The greatest thing in the world is having real "relationships."

My man loves to study Texas white-tailed bucks. He is so passionate about nature. I love that about him! It was deer season a few years ago in Texas and we were celebrating Thanksgiving out of town. That town had a man's dream — a super sporting/hunting goods store. It was getting close to Christmas and the store opened early, so I snuck out of the hotel and went to this store and bought my man a digital game camera that you can hang on a tree, and it takes pictures of any deer that walks by (pretty cool). I couldn't wait to give it to him at Christmas.

Well, as it happens to any normal family around the holidays, stress was knocking on our front door, and we answered it. By the time we got home from our Thanksgiving festivities, we were ready to throw a turkey at each other, and of course, I wanted to take that game camera back to the "guy store" because he darn sure didn't deserve it (in my mind, anyway).

Then (it's always the 'then' that gets you), a voice inside me said, "Put the camera in his truck tonight."

What? "I don't think so!" I said to myself, but I knew the next morning, before daylight, he would be heading out for a day of doing what he loves: being out in nature, studying and hunting the great Texas white-tailed deer. With that in mind and the voice inside me telling me to do something for him that I didn't think he deserved, I went with something that was way beyond me. I did the opposite of what I felt like doing.

I wrote my man a note that went something like this: "If I had no tomorrows, I would want to give you all I had today." Love, Joy

I am sure when he got in his truck that morning, heading out for his hunt, he was just as confused as I was, as to how I could give him this camera before Christmas, and on top of that, when I was totally ticked at him.

We had been through some major life-altering hurdles in our short eight-year marriage, and we both understood how quickly life could be swept away from us. Since then, we have both stepped beyond ourselves and done things for each other that neither one of us earned or deserved at the time, but something inside of us said, "If I had no tomorrow, I would want to give you all I had today."

Come with me to Hebrews 3:13

But encourage one another daily, Truly, we all need encouragement daily! **as long as it is called Today,** Today may be all you have or all that your family member, a friend, a co-worker, or even a stranger may have. Give all you have today! **so that none of you may be hardened by sin's deceitfulness.** The less we do for one another, the more we look inward and the more we are deceived. We were created out of relationship. We were meant to have real relationships.

What I learned:

WOW, this is one of my favorites because I realize how much God has been changing me. I am not sure I will ever have the relationship thing to perfection because I am human. I was born with a sinful nature that started when Eve ate the apple. Basically, it's in the genes, but I can do my best to listen to the voice that tells me the opposite of what my little sinful self wants to do. When I listen to the voice of truth, I end up "giving all I have today" because, what if I have no tomorrows?

Your turn in the Word:

"I know that there is nothing better for men than to be _____ and _____ good while they live" (Ecclesiastes 3:12).

_____

_____

_____

Thinking of Others ...

Giver of life, help us to go beyond ourselves and look to you for direction in our relationships. Let us look outside our circumstances and listen to your voice directing us to your truth for our steps Today. God, I pray for those listed below, that you will help me give them all I have Today.

_____

_____

_____

Repentance ...

Re- in repent is something I understand. I keep having to re-repent for my actions and choices that don't line up with who you are. Lord, forgive me for handling relationships my way and not yours. Forgive me for not listening to your voice of truth. Doing what I want always leads me down roads I don't want to go, whether now or later.

_____

_____

_____

My Desires ...

God of Mercy, thank You for "giving me all you have today." You are always so faithful to give me everything I need. I want to be just like you. I want to be able to see needs and fulfill them Today for you and for all other relationships that you have placed in my life.

_____

_____

_____

Today? Yes, today! What would you give to someone today if you had no tomorrows?

Give it!

Day #35:
CLOSETS OF LIFE

The Sense of Humor Spot:

A young businessman had just started his own company. He'd rented a beautiful office and had it furnished with antiques. Sitting there, he saw a man come into the outer office. Wishing to appear busy, the businessman picked up the phone and started to pretend he had a big deal working. He threw huge figures around and made giant commitments. Finally, he hung up and asked the visitor, "Can I help you?"

The man said, "Sure. I've come to install the phone!"

WORD

Cleaning out — those two words make me cringe every time I hear them. No matter how good it feels when it's finally done, cleaning out (especially closets — can I hear an "Amen" from all my girls?!) is a process and so is cleaning out our closet called life!

I recently heard about a girl who loved organizing closets, drawers, and anything in the home. I truly couldn't imagine why she loved it, but I guess we all have our gifts. Closets sure aren't my calling! As a matter of fact, I will avoid it for years. I may do a little here and there to make myself feel a little better, but I never maintain a lifestyle of a "clean closet." I couldn't find anything in there, and besides, by hiring her, I was letting her use her gift! So enough was enough, and I called the trooper closet cleaner in. I just knew her price was right.

As she arrived, I was so excited to greet her, get her in the house, lock her in so she couldn't leave, and take her immediately to the massive, multiplying pile of chaotic mess a girl can compile over months of avoiding herself.

Can I just say a closet is a place we have to go every day? It begins our day and ends our day. It needs our attention. Just as our closets are a place we begin and end our day, so it is with the closets of our lives. The closet of our lives need attention daily, otherwise we will be wearing "some issue" that doesn't "fit" us, or carrying "bags" (the things of this world we were never meant to carry) that weigh us down.

So, I will get to the point, we talked about how "we" were going to take everything totally out of the closet, then clean it, wiping off the shelves, vacuuming, etc. Then "we" were going to go through what "I" want and will keep, put that back in the closet, and give the rest away.

I had to stop her and question why "I" and "we" were cleaning the closet. I called the trooper closet cleaner in so I wouldn't have to clean out the closet ... I wanted her to do it for me!

I didn't want to do the work on my closet! Just as I resist wanting to clean my clothes closet, it is the same when it comes to my "life" closet. I just want someone else to clean up my mess. When I am the one cleaning my own mess, that is when I really get the "message" of what I do want in my closet and the things or people that don't fit me anymore. I need to clean out my "life" closet. No one else can decide who or what fits your lifestyle as it changes and hopefully grows into a more positive and beautiful life each year as changes come and go.

So I thought about cutting the strings, unlocking the door, and releasing the trooper closet cleaner from her "gifted" duties. Then I realized she could help guide me. She may not be able to go through the process of deciding what I wanted to keep or throw away, but she could help me make some good decisions. It reminds of the scripture in Ecclesiastics 4:9 that says, "Two are better than one, because they have a good return for their work."

She had great ideas, she knew where things should go, she knew how to direct me when I was running to the kitchen for another "break" (OK, I'm an emotional eater), and she also gave me the inspiration I needed to do the work!

Her time had come to an end. She had to get home to fix dinner for her family (if that tells you anything about how long the "process" took)! When she left, I had a few things to hang up and shoe rack to buy, but the best part was getting everything in its place. Now the fun part: I got to decorate! Yes, I decorated my closet.

I hung mirrors, pictures, used the rod on one of my shelves to hang my necklaces, I even ended up with a very little spot to iron clothes! In case anyone is wondering, this closet looks like a bowling alley, only a lot shorter! A girl never has enough closet space!

In the end, I got to decorate my clothes closet because I had made space by going through my mess. The message I walked away with was one that I will carry in my bag of hope for the rest of my life. I realized when I clean out the things and people that don't fit my life, I have to do some "life cleaning" in order to open up space to decorate my life the way I want it. I don't stuff stuff and people in there that I have to see every day when they no longer fit.

We really have more control over what gets in our lives than we will acknowledge!

Come with me to Hebrews 12:11

No discipline seems pleasant at the time, but painful. Yes, cleaning out both your clothes closet and your "life closet" takes discipline and is very painful. It doesn't seem even remotely pleasant. **Later on, however, it produces a harvest of righteousness and peace for those who have been trained by it.** When I walk in my clean closet that is organized, I can actually see the floor and know what I have or don't have. It brings peace and a feeling of being right for me and my life.

What I learned:

I really want a clean, organized closet to get dressed in everyday and a clean, organized "life closet" to live out each day. I think we all do, but sometimes we want someone else to clean up our mess, organize our things, put people in lives, or take people out of our lives. In reality, I am the only one who is able to take full responsibility for myself. I have to decide what I will wear, who I will surround myself with and how much baggage I will allow myself to carry.

Your turn in the Word:

"The end of _____ things is near. Therefore be _____ minded and self-controlled so that you can pray" (1 Peter 4:7).

_____

_____

_____

Thinking of Others ...

Because you love us, Lord, you protect us by giving us your Holy Spirit to guide us. You tell us when something or someone doesn't fit us or in the closets of our lives. Jesus, help us to trust you and not to "wear" what we want, but wear what pleases you and let only those people in our lives that you want us to let into our innermost private areas of our lives ... our life closets!

Repentance ...

Lord, in Proverbs 28:13 it says, "He who conceals his sins does not prosper, but whoever confesses and renounces them finds mercy." God of truth, I confess I have things in the closet of my life that I need to clean out. Reveal the root of my sins so that I may please you, find your mercy, and prosper.

My Desires ...

God of mercy, I want a "life closet" that, at any time, you can look in, and I won't be ashamed at the things or people that are in there. I want to have a teachable spirit and a desire to listen and obey your promptings when you are trying to help me make those decisions on who or what I let in my "life closet."

Girlfriend, don't be overwhelmed. Just ask a friend over who is a great organizer and ask her to help you go through your clothes, your shoes, or whatever else needs some organizing to bring peace to your life.

Now, ask a friend to come over who has the kind of relationship with God that you would like in your life. Ask her to help you go through the baggage you have collected and help you replenish those things or people with what and who God wants in your life.

Day #36:
DON'T YOU JUDGE ME, EARL!

The Sense of Humor Spot:

There were three ladies standing around talking about their funerals. One said, "I hope when people look at me they say I was a humanitarian, a devoted woman of faith."

The second woman said, "I hope people look at me and say I was a great teacher, doctor, and a wonderful mother."

I HOPE WHEN PEOPLE LOOK AT ME...

The third woman said, "I hope when people look at me, they say, 'I think I see something moving.'"

WORD

I have always loved this saying, "Don't you judge me, Earl." It came from a TV show, and the characters all lived pretty messed up lives. One of the characters always said to her ex-husband, "Don't you judge me, Earl," as she was knee deep in straight-up sin!

Those four words, "don't you judge me" have so much substance and depth in them. This is so vital in keeping our community in harmony. See, if I knew of all the junk in your trunk, and you knew all the junk in my trunk, we would pretty much run from one another. That is the problem. We all have junk, but I think that is where it should stay — in the trunk.

I've learned to look and admire what I see today in others. I also decided long ago not to go looking for a booger, because if I look for one long enough, I will find one — and besides, it's so unladylike.

Keeping score, judging, condemning, conditioning my personality to impress those I want to impress, and treating those closest to me like a piece of yesterday's news, compared to the attention and time I give to others, have all turned out to be life-suckers for me. They suck the life right out of me and the energy out of my relationships.

As far as I know, we are all sinners, and we all need some amazing grace. Giving one another chances to make new choices is the greatest gift we could give each other and ourselves. With every "thing" and every "person," there are times when you have to just walk away. Only God changes things and people; we can't.

Now that being said, if I see a friend or even a foe, for that matter, going down a road that will lead to the darkest tunnel of their lives, I might try to give them some hope and loving wisdom. I can only pray that when I try to give them a word of hope or wisdom, that they know I am sharing out of love and not condemnation or judgment and that they will hear it that way.

Have you ever been talking to someone, and they are not giving you the time of day, or they are convicting you with their eyes? Whether you're a businessperson on top of the world, making tons of money, or you're the bum on the street, you don't know the blood and sweat that businessperson went through to get there or what that bum lost (innocence, family) to get there.

I have learned that God can give and take away in an instant. I have also learned a condemning spirit is the quickest way to lose family, friends, and even strangers. A word doesn't even have to be spoken; our facial expressions give it away almost every time.

Comparing could fall under the umbrella of judging. If I am looking at someone else's life, and taking in information on what I see, and then comparing my life to theirs it really is judging — putting value upon one or another.

Learning not to judge or compare my life to someone else's life has been a tough thing to keep in check, because I look at one friend, and she may have an awesome career, but her family doesn't ever see her. One friend seems to have it all (kids, the house, the cars), yet her husband doesn't even know she exists.

Every time I have judged or compared my life to someone else, I lose! I lose sight of how awesome of a life God has given me! Now, I totally believe in taking the good from all my friends and learning from them. Comparisons can be good when I want to be my best for God. The best place to begin and end in comparing myself is by learning, understanding, and knowing the true character of God. After all, he has all the coolest qualities: he never rejects me, he has the greatest sense of humor, he knows exactly who to connect me to and when, and he is the great "I AM."

Making false statements and judging one another are, well, just plain wrong, and they are some of the worst things we could ever do to each other. I have not been where someone else has been. If I haven't seen it for myself, it's not my job to talk about it or judge someone before I even know them. I have no idea how a person was raised, who denied them, abused them, abandoned them, or the lack of guidance in their lives, which lead to poor, poor choices. I don't know where they have been.

Using clear thinking and common sense to decide where and who I will spend my time with will be a great way to keep me around those with godly character.

Therefore ... "Don't you judge me, Earl," and I won't judge you!

Come with me to Matthew 7:3

"Why do you look at the speck of sawdust in your brother's eye
Or, why do we judge and talk about our family, friends, or even strangers'

"issues"? and pay no attention to the plank in your own eye? Sometimes we can see so clearly another's "issues' when at the same time our "stuff" is like having a telephone pole hanging out of our own eye. Yet we would rather talk about their "issues" rather than making sure we take care of our own.

What I Learned:

This day's devotional has been a tough one because while I am writing this, I think of a moment yesterday where I was comparing myself. I was not really judging in a critical way, but I was looking at someone and drawing my own "conclusions" based on appearances.

OK, so I guess that might have been judging, but I judged on the positive side. Truly, this is a tough temptation to keep in check. I always have to remember to compare and judge myself according to God's character, not men. When I do this, I know I am good to go, and I don't have to look to anyone else to see if I measure up.

Your turn in the Word:

"You, therefore, have no excuse, you who pass _____ on someone else, for at whatever point you _____ the other, you are condemning _____, because you who pass judgment do the same things" (Romans 2:1).

_____

_____

_____

Thinking of Others ...

Peacemaker, you did not ever intend for us to turn on one another, judge one another, or compare one another. Lord, give us the desire to give to others the grace we so desperately need and want in the portion we want grace to be given to us.

_____

_____

_____

Repentance ...

Lord of love, let your mercy fall on my foolish words that have hurt or judged another. God, I get it wrong. Before I know it I am comparing and judging to see how I measure up. Please forgive me for wasting the precious time you have given me. I choose to give mercy and grace to others and myself.

_____

_____

_____

My Desires ...

My Protector, I know you have all these wonderful plans, principles, and precepts — in place and active — to protect me. I want to run into the arms of your truth daily, so I am not so easily swayed into the judging, comparing, and condemning that I don't want any part of. Give me your heart of mercy and grace for everyone you place in my life.

_____

_____

_____

How often do I look at others to judge or compare? Who do I judge and compare myself with?

When was the last time you focused on who God is — in other words, on his character? Write three things about God's character.

Day #37:
PARTIAL LIGHT

The Sense of Humor Spot:
"Why is it that when we talk to God, we're praying, but when God talks to us, we're schizophrenic?"
— Lily Tomlin

WORD

Do you ever just get a revelation that you wish you could ignore, but the reality is, you are one French fry short of a Happy Meal? That is, you feel like something is missing, and it could be as little as one French fry (one bad habit), but this one small "thing" is keeping you from a true Happy Meal called "Life."

Here is one of the most revealing stories about my walk in true light with one true God. I was heading to the laundry room on a cold, winter night. I had been thinking about writing this devotional book and I was looking for God lessons. He is always trying to teach me ("stubborn" and "mule" come to my mind, for some reason). So, I go to flip the light switch on and I got nothing. Not one but both of the lights in my laundry room went out at the very same time. Talk about timing. And I am not just talking about light bulbs. I knew in that moment that God was teaching me his lesson, his way.

He knows just how to get my attention. I couldn't see anything. I was in totally darkness, and I needed to get the laundry I had in the washer out. You know how towels have that moldy smell if you leave them overnight in the washing machine (it took me a while to figure that one out)! Thankfully, I did have a hall light working. So I turned it on. The light from the hallway was "enough" to see, but not enough to "really see."

Yup, you guessed it, here comes the God lesson: At this particular time I was struggling with the same "issue" of wanting to do things my way instead of God's way. As I was doing the laundry, I felt as though it was God's way of showing me that, yes, I was letting "some" light in and seeing him working in my life. I was having an ongoing relationship with him, but I couldn't fully see with the bright light that he wanted me to see with because of the sin (issue) that I was letting get in the way of truly seeing all that he is and all that he wants me to be.

Sin is sin, no matter how big or small. It just is. Sure, I can get away with it for now, but sin always reveals itself. It manifests itself eventually, and no matter what type of sin it is, it comes with a cost.

Sin is when I do something I know God is telling me not to do. (It doesn't matter what someone else is doing.) If God is against it, so should I be. Sin has some origin (source that it starts from) in my heart, and it's so much easier to keep my heart clean than it is to clean it after I have tainted it. I can't fight my fleshly appetite by indulging it. It's like wanting to lose weight and eating a gallon of ice cream at every meal. It doesn't work. I have to understand that I need people in my circle who are truly serving God, because those who don't serve God will not help me serve Him. Most importantly, I can't fight fleshly temptations with fleshly weapons. So what do I fight sin with? I'm glad you asked!

The s-Word and more BS!

God is faithful. He will not leave me when I am struggling with sin. He will help me overcome. But there are choices I have to make. Sometimes the easiest way to end a relationship with sin is to just drop it. Get away from it. There was sin in my past I thought I would never overcome, but I have, with the help of calling on the Master Healer and making choices that would give me V-I-C-T-O-R-Y!

Come with me to I John 1:7

But if If I choose. I have a choice. God will never override my choices. I walk in free will. That is why I want his will, not mine. My will, well, it is too free! **we walk in the light,** Light is a beautiful thing. Light cannot live in darkness. That within itself is beautiful. **as he is in the light,** God is the light at the end of the tunnel. He is our way to see in darkness, in our circumstances. Light brings life. Just ask the trees and plants in the spring what makes them grow. **we have fellowship with one another,** Fellow-ship — I need you and you need me. We are on this ship of life together, and the most encouraging thing to know is that someone is there. **and the blood of Jesus, his Son, purifies us from all sin.** When Jesus lowered himself from being the King of kings in heaven to sitting on a throne and came down to this earth, to be tortured and nailed on a cross, while dying on that cross for you and me, he said, "It is finished." He lived and died on this earth for us. He shed his blood, so that we could be free from all sin through him. Jesus finished it!

What I Learned:

I learned that I can have total victory in Jesus Christ. I also learned I have some maturing to do, some choices to make, and some dying to my fleshly desires to take care of. I understand that those things "I think" I want to do are only things that eventually break my heart and leave me feeling more guilty and empty. After reading in 1 John 1:7 that Jesus can purify me from all my sins, I realize it's just like anything else. It is a constant process: working, learning, growing, nurturing, and then resting in God's rewards.

Your turn in the Word:

"Your word is a lamp to my feet and a _____ for my path" (Psalms 119:105).

_____

_____

_____

Thinking of Others ...

Jesus, sweet and humble Jesus, thank You for coming down to this earth to rescue us from our sinful natures. Lord, we know the only way to eternity is through you and by believing in the blood that you shed for us.

_____

_____

_____

Repentance ...

God, I am so embarrassed and so ashamed that I lose sight of who you are and all that you have done to set me free. You sent your one and only Son to die on a cross for me, my friends, my family, and everyone one who chooses to believe in you. I don't want to choose sin over you. I choose your will, your way!

_____

_____

My Desires ...

Mercy of God, rain down on us. Give the ones I love, the ones I don't know, and the ones that don't know you a hunger for righteousness. Let us want to be purified from sin. Help us to want to live in fellowship with one another and have real relationships with each other and with you!

Where am I letting partial darkness in? What light (scripture and repentance) can I expose my sin to?

Day #38:
VISION

The Sense of Humor Spot:
"Where lipstick is concerned, the important thing is not color, but to accept God's final word on where your lips end."
— Jerry Seinfeld

WORD

A quick story (OK, so it's shorter when I tell it). Lin, my husband, has been trying to get me to go up this hill behind our house for years. He

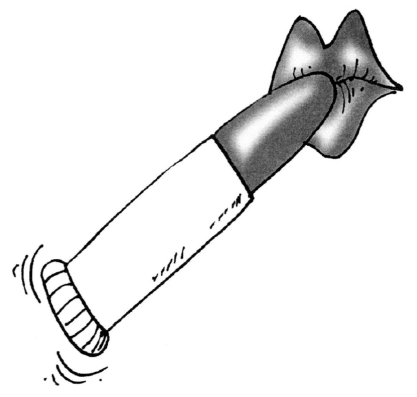

is the woodsy-type guy. The hill is very dense with brush, trees, and covered with creepy crawly things (in my mind, anyway)!

Finally, one day I put on my big girl panties and walked through the thick green "things" and thorns with the determination of a great white-tail hunter.

As I grew comfortable with the mission, I started seeing these beautiful trees that were hidden from all the overgrowth. Three trees in particular (elm and beautiful oak trees) were clumped together with a huge opening. Mental note to self: This would be an awesome place to put a play area/ sanctuary-type getaway. The sweet deer had made their winding trails through this wilderness (home to them).

As we followed the natural paths, we reached the "Walter Payton Hill," so Lin likes to call it. Walter Payton was known for putting on his cleats and training on hills. Why? Because hills are steep, and the under-brush is U.G.L.Y.! You want to get in shape? Come try her out! So we climbed the "W.P.H." Needless to say, afterwards we needed an oxygen mask and a chair. At that point, I settled for a stump. After recovering, I turned around and looked down from the hill that we just conquered.

Guess what I saw? A vision: At that moment, I realized that all along we had a jewel in our own backyard, but I hadn't been willing to go through the brush, thorns, and crawly things to see it! You know those times when someone or something is trying to nudge you to the "next level," but your lack of willingness won't let you go there?

All you see is thorns in the path. It's too confusing and too over-whelming to see past where you already made your home, your refuge. You're comfortable where you are. You know what I mean: It's not "great," but you rationalize that it's good, knowing all along there's "something" missing, more to this life.

Lin couldn't "make me" go higher to see the "vision." I had to decide for myself. I needed to see what he was trying to show me. I had to decide that I was willing to go through the thorns (the things that have made my heart bleed), the thick green stuff (the experiences I didn't understand), the creepy crawly things (the situations or relationships that were snakes in my garden) to see the vision.

Finally, I realized that Lin is a man of wisdom. I trust him. I decided to follow him up that hill. Step by step, rock by rock, discovering the "purpose," the "vision," for each thorn, each "green thing" that I previ-ously couldn't understand or identify. Why were we placed in this home with the "W.P.H." behind us? God is showing me, even today, that he is going to use this land for his glory!

The point is, you can have all the knowledge in the world, but you are going to have to have the courage to walk through the valley (the self-talk of lies) to the mountain of truth (you are the salt of the earth, the light of the world), and SEE the VISION that GOD has for YOU!

I know it's hard to go to a quiet place and "just listen," but it's in the silent whispers that God gives vision. I had to go to the top of that hill!

COME WITH ME TO HABAKKUK 2:2

Then the Lord replied: **"Write down** I remember things so much better when I write them down. **the revelation** What has been revealed to you? What has God shown you about himself, his creation, or yourself? Write it down, no matter how odd or irrational it may seem to you. **and make it plain on tablets** Don't complicate this. Just write down your raw thoughts on raw paper. **so that a herald may run with it."** Write it so plainly that if a stranger, a royal messenger, or even an angel were to see and hear you write it down, they could go to God and say, "She has the vision. She has written it down. She trusts you, God!"

WHAT I LEARNED:

Stop, trust, and follow GOD'S WISDOM!
Step by step,
Rock by rock,
IT'S MY DECISION!
HE'S just waiting
To give me THE VISION for my life!

YOUR TURN IN THE WORD:

"Trust in the Lord with _____ your heart and lean not on _____ own understanding; in all your ways acknowledge _____, and He will make your paths straight" (Proverbs 3:5-6).

_____

_____

_____

Thinking of Others ...

God, create in us a desire to go higher. To go through the thorns and bushes, the things that hurt us, and take us to your mountaintop. Reveal to us the vision you have for our lives. We want you, your vision, and your plan!

_____

_____

_____

Repentance ...

King of kings, you see me take my same ol' path, over and over again. I want to follow you, your ways, and your path. That path may not seem like the easiest one, but it is the right one. Forgive me for choosing any other path than the path that you already have for me.

_____

_____

_____

My Desires ...

Visionary — that is what you are, obviously. I mean, look at this place! You have done such a beautiful job with your creation: this earth, the people, the mountains, the oceans, the stars, my man, my kids, my family. God, I long to totally trust you in a way that is so clear that I can just look down on my situation and the people and my life and be able to see the vision, the plan you have.

_____

_____

_____

Write the vision down for your life. Don't worry about details or making sense. What is in your heart? What do you dream about doing, being, or having that would bring glory to God?

Everything starts with some sort of vision, even if it's fuzzy!

Day #39:
TIME

The Sense of Humor Spot:
Reaching the end of a job interview, the Human Resources person asked a young engineer who was fresh out of MIT, "What starting salary were you thinking about?"

The engineer said, "In the neighborhood of $125,000 a year, depending on the benefits package."

The interviewer said, "Well, what would you say to a package of five weeks' vacation, 14 paid holidays, full medical and dental, company matching retirement fund to 50% of salary, and a company car leased every two years ... say, a red Corvette?"

The engineer sat up straight and said, "Wow! Are you kidding?"

The interviewer replied, "Yeah, but you started it."

WORD

There is a gift that you can't see; you're not sure how much you have; you don't know where it goes; it is not up to you how much you have; but it is up to you how to spend it. The greatest gift you can give, spend, or have is quality TIME!

Through surviving breast cancer twice, I've sensed the threat of death; therefore, I have come to realize how precious and valuable time is. The way I share my time, the way I see time, and the way I spend my time. Basically, I have discovered I have to be a steward of my time. God knows I don't have it all figured out, and chances are, neither do you, because your life doesn't come with a manual that says exactly what you are suppose to do with your time, how you are to spend your time, what job to take, which man to marry, which church to go to, what house to buy or how much time to spend on it, how many kids to have or adopt, is it enough to be a stay-at-home mom (YES!) or be a mom and work outside the home, which schools to trust to teach your kids, which friends to stay connected with ... SOMEBODY HELP!!!

There are too many meetings, programs, organizations, and other obligations calling me to do, do, do and go, go, go faster. My life was and still sometimes is detrimentally impacted by these time pressures. The results are debilitating to my relationship with God and with others. I need time to think, meditate, and truly understand God's truth. In this fast-paced society of always being on the go, I end up failing to grasp who I am, why I am here, and where I am really going.

Many times, I have been like the taxi driver who told his passengers, "I have some good news and then some bad news. The bad news is we took a wrong turn and are on the wrong road. But don't worry; the good news is we are making great time." It's as though the going itself, the movement at a fast pace, is its own reward, regardless of where it takes me. But that is nowhere near the truth. God is a God of order. He is a God of timing. He is a God of principles. He gives us all 24 hours a day. It is up to me how I spend the only time I "have" to spend.

Time, and how I use it or abuse it, will eventually take its toll. For me, I spent my girls' infant and toddler years being a worn-out mom and wife, working as a stylist, aerobics instructor, building two houses, and volunteering for anything that I felt pressure to do, along with surviving those two rounds with breast cancer, having a double mastectomy and seven surgeries, along with chemotherapy the first go-round. Then the second time around, I had two more surgeries and radiation. HERE'S YOUR SIGN, JOY!!!

I guess God knew he had to whack me upside the head to get my attention, and apparently I am a slow learner. The world was telling me one thing — go, go, go — and my heart was saying "slow down," your life is about your relationships, not "what you do," but "whose you are."

I am God's, and when I refresh my mind with his word, I come to understand that a child of his was not meant to live a life of worry, rushing, and doing all the time. At the time when I was rushing around, worrying, and doing all those "things," my family was suffering. Obviously, I was suffering, and the only one who could stand up and say, "I have to change how I spend my time" was me. It's the same for you.

Believe me, it has not been an easy choice to go against what my flesh wants, which is for the world to see me spinning 20 different, cool-looking plates at one time. Thankfully, the more I get to know the Lord, the more I don't care what the world thinks. I care what he thinks, and if I get still enough or slow down long enough, I can hear that still, small voice saying, "That's too much. That's not right for you. Or, YES, go enjoy that." I may not get it right every time, but I have come to the realization that listening to the Father of Time is a wise way to use my time.

Come with me to Luke 21:6

"As for what you see here, the time will come when not one stone will be left on another; every one of them will be thrown down." What you see today, the houses, the jobs, the things, all that "stuff" will be gone one day. Why are we striving so much to keep these things when what really matters is our relationship with God? When we get our time, energy, and our lives revolving around his order, his plans, his principles for our lives, things just naturally flow. He is faithful to bring what we need and even sometimes what we want, if it lines up the awesome life he has planned for us!

What I learned:

I have come to the truth that I ("me") am responsible for how I spend the one thing I have to spend every day: my time. No one can force me to make choices for myself unless I let them. Just like everyone else, I have 24 hours every day to spend wasting or producing, worrying or trusting, taking or giving, resenting or loving, whining or singing, wishing or planning. Whatever I do or wherever I may be, it really boils down to the choices I make day in and day out, because they really do add up!

Your turn in the Word:

"But from everlasting to _____ the Lord's love is with those who _____ him, and his righteousness with their children's children-with those who keep his _____ and remember to obey his _____." (Psalm 103:17-18).

_____
_____
_____

Thinking of Others ...
Giver of time, thank you for this gift of life and the 24 hours a day you give each of us to enjoy. Father, help us to choose your path for our lives so that we can enjoy this life (not just grin and bear it) but live

fruitful, happy, fulfilling lives through examining how we spend our time, and without hesitation, change any time-snatcher that steals the life you meant for us to have.

_____

_____

_____

Repentance ...

Oh, the time I have wasted on so many things that weren't your plan for my life! The things I have chased after instead of your truth, your will, your way — so many things to ask forgiveness for, and you know each one. Therefore, from now on, I choose to ask you each day, "OK, I am your vessel — what is your will?" By using common sense and a keeping clear conscience, I know I can spend my time in valuable ways, chasing peace and freedom in your Son, Jesus Christ.

_____

_____

_____

My Desires ...

Creator of time, you are so amazing. You have perfect timing; even the sun knows when to rest, and the stars know when to shine. God, I want that. I want that natural ability to consistently line up with you and your rhythm every single second of time you have given me here on earth.

_____

_____

_____

What is a "time sucker" for you that you know is stealing your joy and peace? When was the last time you spent quality time with God? Your family? Your man? Your children?

If you can't remember, chances are you need to "slow 'er down"!

Day #40:
LIFE IS FAIR

The Sense of Humor Spot:
"Better to remain silent and be thought a fool than to speak out and remove all doubt."
— Abraham Lincoln

WORD

Storms, thunder, lightning bolts, and then comes the rain. Life is fair; it rains on everyone!

We run from the rain, we use umbrellas to protect us, and hopefully build our houses on concrete slabs, otherwise known as a firm foundation. As it rains and storms in nature, it rains and storms in our lives. When storms come into our lives, when an illness sets in your body, your husband says he doesn't love you anymore, you lose a family member, you lose your job, an accident happens, a fire consumes your home, a friend betrays you, your church becomes a battlefield rather than a refuge, your finances are depleted, or even the small things seem big, a few extra pounds, a misunderstanding at work, a mistake of bumping the side of your car ... STORMS, THUNDER, LIGHTING.

Life's issues can feel like it's raining and flooding into your emotional house of pain. It happens to us all. When storms hit in our lives, we have to know what and who our foundation is built upon. What do we believe? What will help us withstand our storms? How do we not fall apart when the rain and the floods of life come? We need a firm foundation. If we were to tell what and who we believe can help us overcome the storms in our lives, we could easily see what our foundations are built upon. When the rains come and life's issues arise, where do you go for shelter? How do you withstand the storms that will come?

When I have built my foundation on other people, believing they were the answer, they could rescue me, I eventually found out they had a life and couldn't be there every minute, encouraging me and protecting me in my storm. They were a great comfort, but they could only cover me for so long. I have also tried to build my foundation on things, money, and my career; yet again, those things could only sustain me for so long. When my "ultimate storm" came, it stripped me of everything I knew to be "my foundation" at the time. My health failed me when I discovered I had breast cancer, and I was facing death (at least that is what it looked and felt like to me, especially during chemotherapy).

We had water damage in our home, I had a double mastectomy (losing my ability as a woman to breastfeed my 6-month-old little girl); I was losing the ability to do my job (it's hard to teach aerobics or cut hair when you can't raise your hands over your head); I lost my hair; and I was scared that I would lose my man's desire for me (but he was there for me and stayed with me through the storms).

I was losing hope, I had a 6-month-old and a three-year-old, both beautiful little girls, who were looking at me with uncertainty, and the final lightning bolt was a pop-up on my computer that said, "What happens if mommy dies?" It was at that moment in my personal storm that I found out I did have a firm foundation.

It was spoken over me by my parents' words years ago and by the s-Words that I have read, studied, and believed all my life. Those s-Words, the truth that I read, believed, and searched out were the "rainbow" after the rain. They were the vibrant colors that kept me going.

It was then that I saw the Son, Jesus Christ, for who he is and has been all my life. I just didn't realize I didn't have to wait until heaven to see him or really know him. I could have a horizontal relationship with him on earth, not a vertical one, where he is up there somewhere. I started talking to God, instead of just reading the Bible. I began to see the s-Word become real in my life.

As I spoke words to God, just like you and I talk to one another, I told him about my worries, my concern for what would happen to my family if I died. I told him I didn't want to leave my family, and he heard my cry. I couldn't help but to seek him like a precious jewel for being so faithful to me and giving me amazing grace that I didn't deserve. When I became a true seeker for myself by spending time studying him through his word, (the Bible), learning his plans, his principles, his precepts, his Truth, and as I began to have a "real" relationship with him, I began to see the ways he even cares about the littlest details in my life. He gives himself. Building my life upon his word and truly coming into a relationship with him, I know I can withstand any storm because he is my firm foundation.

Why do we wait until there is a storm to seek out shelter for our lives? He is the shelter that will always protect and withstand any storm with you!

Come with me to Matthew 7:25

The rain came down, Rain (issues) will come in our lives. **the streams rose,** Our lives will have issues that just keep rising. **and the winds blew** We will feel the winds of confusion, hurt, and pain. **and beat against that house;** Those "things," "people," and "issues" will beat against your house called life. **yet it did not fall,** This is the beauty of God. This is one of his promises of being a seeker of him, a follower of his word. **because it had its foundation on the Rock.** There is eternal life; you will live forever in eternity when you build your life on the firm foundation of the King of kings, his s-Word, and his Son, Jesus Christ.

What I learned:

I learned that God sent his only son, Jesus Christ, to live and die on this earth so that we may have eternal life, if we build our lives on his firm foundation. We build our lives by the choices we make each day. I am also encouraged to know that I don't have to survive the rain, the winds, the lightning and thunder of life's issues on my own. When Jesus Christ died and ascended into heaven, God was so faithful to leave another part of who he is — Holy Spirit — here, living on earth, inside you and me, helping us build our lives on a firm foundation.

You learn and understand all these things as you become a seeker and surrender your life to a great and mighty God who created you and me, the oceans, the trees, the stars, the mountains, the animals, and the planet earth, through words. Words have power. You create your life, your foundation, with the words you speak and the words you believe!

Your turn in the Word:

"Command those who are rich in this present world not to be arrogant nor to put their _____ in _____, which is so uncertain, but to put their _____ in _____, who richly provides us with _____ for our enjoyment. Command them to do good, to be rich in good _____, and to be generous and willing to share. In this way they will lay up treasure for themselves as a firm _____ for the coming age, so that they may take hold of the life that is _____ life" (I Timothy 6: 17-19).

_____

_____

_____

Thinking of Others ...

By your grace, God, help us build our lives on a firm foundation in you. Help us to understand the true riches of this world which are stored up and brought forth out of our relationship with you. Give us the understanding and wisdom to know you can shelter us through any storm by believing in who you are, your word, and your active Spirit living within us.

_____

_____

_____

Repentance ...

Shelter in the storms of life, you have been so faithful. You have taken me out of the earthquakes I have created through my own foolish actions and choices. Thank you for the rainbows colored with vibrant hope after the showers of despair. You alone are all I want and need. Forgive me for not choosing you over the people, places, and things that I have run to instead of you. I turn to you because you are my rock-solid Foundation when everything else is gone.

_____

_____

_____

My Desires ...

My refuge, my creator, I know you know the beginning from the end. You are the way, the truth, and the light. Your word is power, and I want to run to the arms of your grace and speak words that create the life you have planned for me. Not my foolish ways, Lord, but your firm foundation. God, like a tree planted by the waters, give me a root system that is so deep, wide, and full of nutrients that I produce fruit in abundance according to your word.

_____

_____

_____

What storm or storms are you facing today? Who or what are you trusting to get you through these storms?

How do you want to rebuild after the storm? What or WHO will you build your life on?